© A. Karl / J. Kemp, 1991

Also by Roger Burke

Novels
The Last Cowboy (1972)
The Out Post Cafe (1974)
A Nice Place To Die (1975)
Beyond Their Country (1976)
The Last Train To Bregenz (1982)
A Home In Bohemia (1991)
The Last Good City (1992)

Collected Stories
Such Young Men (1976)
And Other Americans (1980)

Collected Essays
From The Front (1980)
After Boise There's Pocatello (1988)

Books
Jack Hurley: the last boxing manager alive (1972)

A HOME IN BOHEMIA

by Roger Burke

Columbia River Book Co.,
3404 S. Auburn
Kennewick,Wash 99337

Copyright (c) 1995 Columbia River Book Co.,
3404 S. Auburn
Kennewick,Washington 99337, USA
tel: (509)-582-3953
Cover Illustration by Carlos Vigil
Copyright by Carlos Vigil and Columbia River Book Co.,

Printed in the United States of America
First edition 1995
Library of Congress Catalog Card Number 95-067929
ISBN 0-9623556-1-5

All rights including reproduction of by
photographic or electronic processes and
translation into other languages are fully
reserved under the International Copyright
Union and International Copyright Convention.

This book is sold subject to the condition
that it shall not be re-sold or otherwise
circulated in any other form without the
publisher's prior consent.

CARLOS VIGIL   Illustrator/artist

The illustrations on pages xiv, 24, 60, 86, 138, 196, and 202 are the work
of Mr. Vigil.

He was born in Capuun, Colorado, March 21, 1935. He has been married
for the last 38 years to his wife Carol. He is widely known in the Pacific
Northwest as one of the finest illustrators in the region.

This book is dedicated to the memory of Dr. Milada Horakova

Special Acknowledgement

This book couldn't have been written without the help of many people in Plzen, such as Svetla B., Alena S., and many other persons too numerous to mention in this space, but whose spiritual generosity gave me understanding and admiration for Bohemia, its history and people.

With special thanks to Annette Bowden for technical support.

Introduction

In light of the fact this book is planned for publication in Eastern Europe, following publication in the United States, it is necessary to write an introduction not only about its author but to include some history that cannot be found in American history books.

It is well-known in Russia and Eastern Europe that under the communist regimes the only history permitted to be published and taught in schools was that approved of by political apparatchiks. This brought about a condition known as "blank spots." It also gave birth to the term "non-person." Dissidents who couldn't be "rehabilitated" simply ceased to exist in official records. Their names were purged from history books. The result was a cultural mutation whose effects cannot be calculated. Something of the same thing evolved in America following World War II with the same results that today are impossible to calculate.

These "blank spots" in American history are only recently coming to light by the declassification of official documents that tell how badly the American government errored, and in many cases how the establishment press, covered up government immorality. In other cases, such as events in Eastern Europe, documents were classified or even destroyed to protect reputations of well-known American politicians. It became clear after the end of World War II those who resisted this official and un-official policy were persona non grata. For example, in 1946 George Orwell's classic tale Animal Farm was rejected by the first 12 American publishers on political grounds. Countless other writers without Mr. Orwell's literary fame were rejected and became "non-persons."

"The novel is the eternal battlefield of good versus evil," Ernest Hemingway said.

Yet since the end of World War II American literature has not only declined in quality but has lost all contact with moral issues. George Orwell correctly stated the case: "Everything in our age conspires to turn the writer, and every other kind of artist as well, into a minor official, working on themes handed down from above and never telling what seems to him the whole of the truth...What is really at issue is the right to report contemporary events truthfully."

Even in American universities there are subjects considered taboo. In July of 1990 Edward Hoagland, a professor at Bennington College in the state of Vermont, wrote an essay for a well-known American magazine, Esquire, under the title "Shhh! Our Writers Are Sleeping! (or have they just fallen into a deep moral coma?)" Mr. Hoagland's, essay so infuriated some establishment types, demonstrations were orchestrated against him at his college and for a time he was actually suspended. Perhaps Mr. Hoagland's unforgivable sin was the truthful comment, "I believe establishment writers in one place would be establishment writers in another and that the apparatchiks who speed up or slow careers in a totalitarian system would hold the same positions here." His comment is unforgivable because it brings to light the role of "thought police" in American life.

I am trying to help readers in Eastern Europe understand that just as their best writers were harassed and silenced by apparatchiks of one brand our most courageous writers have been, and still are, muzzled by another brand of apparatchiks. By bringing such an unsavory subject up in public, Mr. Hoagland made himself a target. And he very nearly became a "non-person." Other American dissident writers have not been so lucky.

The Russian poet Yevtushenko wrote, "The best people under Stalin were pruned away. It was like a nightmare in which a gang determined to kill all the Thoroughbred horses and wandered through the stables at night with axes. Horses as a bred survived, but many of them turned out to be horses with the psychology of mice. We need to do much to be able to restore our human bred."

A HOME IN BOHEMIA is to be sure a story about historical events and people in Eastern Europe. But it is also a story about one American, David Wilson. Paraphrasing Ernest Hemingway it is, "the eternal story of good versus evil." But A HOME IN BOHEMIA is also a story of hope. "Affirmation conforms with our natural feeling. Negation contradicts it. Affirmation invites us to be at home in this world and to throw ourselves voluntarily into action; negation requires that we live in the world as strangers and that we choose a passive role. By its very nature ethics is affiliated with affirmation. **One must be active if one is** to serve the ideal of Good." - Dr. Albert Schweitzer, The Evolution of Ethics.

David Wilson, is a trade mark central character in all novels written by Roger Burke, because Wilson is a man afflicted by ideals of affirmation which force him to take sides in the struggle of good versus evil. Wilson, like Dr. Schweitzer, instinctively knows a man cannot be passive in the world and serve "the ideal of good." This transforms Wilson from a passive role in the world to the role of an activist.

It is this quality that generates hope in the novels of Burke. Yevtushenko was so right; we must do much to restore our human breed. We promised and believed after War II that never again would the civilized world permit another Holocaust, but in these last years we have witnessed the "ethnic cleansing" by the Serbs in Bosnia and NATO and the United Nations have proven to be giants with the "psychology of mice" too timid to defend either innocent life or the very principles in their charter. And these were the organizations that were going to defend civilization!

This passive failure of morals has spread into every cell of modern life and is the root cause for our inner foreboding of the future.

But the writing of Roger Burke, and other dissident writers, cracks the membrane of our gloom. Their spiritual call to us is that we can actively resist evil, that we can fight it hand to hand, if need be, and their message provides us hope.

I've known Roger Burke for over a quarter of a century. One of the remarkable qualities about him as a man and writer is that none of his core values has been eroded or altered by events. That might not seem remarkable until you consider what it means to be a dissident and non-person in a free society. It means for one thing your status is that of an invisible person. That means you cannot defend yourself from those who equate lack of power to lack of skill when just the opposite is the reality - those who write the truth skillfully are feared and those who reinforce the status quo are promoted.

I recall numerous people advising Burke to compromise with the establishment to get his foot in the door and then return to his principles and write what he believed in. His answer was always the same, "If writers in Russia and Eastern Europe can go to prison for their principles, the least I can do is support them by not selling out here."

Yet, being human Burke must have had doubts whether justice would ever be served in his time, just as he must have secretly doubted the day would ever come when Eastern Europe would be free of communism in his life-time. And just as the revolution caught everyone by surprise, I sense the day is coming ever closer that the dissident writers, such as Roger Burke, who have been forced into non-person status for so long, will have their justice served on this side of the Atlantic.

For even in America, much slower than Eastern Europe to change, change is coming. The understanding is slowly filtering down to the man in the street that the status quo is not only not healthy, but bound up in its secrecy and censorship it is the enemy of free men. Eastern Europeans understood that reality long before the revolution in 1989.

But the wisdom of another dissident writer, Vaclav Haval must be weighed and understood before a real renaissance can revitalize American life. Speaking before the Czechoslovakian people in January, 1990, after being elected president, Havel captured a truth that extends to all cultures in the post World War II industrial world. "The worst thing is that we are living in a decayed moral environment. We have become morally ill, because we have become accustomed to saying one thing and thinking another. We have learned not to believe in anything, not to have consideration for one another and only to look after ourselves."

The dissident writer derives his power and moral authority by sacrificing his own security to defend principles - as Havel did under the communists. Dissidents writers here sacrificed their security as well and only the most naive failed to understand the establishment would reject their work and consign them to exile on the fringes of society. Without an economic base for support, let alone survival needs, American society is the harshest of landscapes. The dissident who can survive both the economic and spiritual exile in America is something of a miracle in the same way the dissidents who survived the gulags and labor camps in Eastern Europe. The spiritual life of the dissident is thus elevated to a higher plane and it hones his instinct to find truth, where those approved of by the establishment are blind to moral decay.

To find a true dissident writer in American society, one who actually survived without compromise for a period extending any significant time, is as rare as finding a "Thoroughbred" who survived the Stalinist hit men with their axes. But it is only those kind of men, Havel, Solzhenitsyn, and our dissidents, who can be listened to with trust. For they have earned our trust by personal sacrifices. Now it is up to American book publishers to muster the same courage and support our writers with records of telling the truth at risk to their security. If we cannot do that at so little risk of treasure, security and comfort for those who sacrificed their own treasure, security and comfort, then we are unworthy of renaissance and will continue to sink in the moral decay Vaclav Havel spoke of. I am hopeful, however, that it is the activist spirit, the David Wilsons among us, who will prevail and ignite a renaissance.

Richard J. Johnson Ph.D

A HOME IN BOHEMIA

"If anything can cure the world and make mankind pure and whole again, it is the actions and sufferings of those who refused to be bent or bought, who were more willing to lose their lives than their humanity."

- Herman Hesse (1948)

Chapter 1

Wilson was alone in life.
From a distance he appeared to be running away from a large orange ball that the sun made as it set over the desert and behind the humped hills that were the Rattlesnake Mountains.
He did not fight the final 400 yards of the four mile run, as he

4   A HOME IN BOHEMIA

once did, he simply finished his run at an even pace. He wasn't in the shape he was ten years earlier or five years before or even two years before. And he knew it. But he told himself that it was still possible to fight himself into good condition once again.

It wasn't hot yet in the desert. It was April and after walking for several hundred yards over asphalt in a parking lot of a shopping mall, Wilson was breathing normally again and he wiped away the lines of sweat on his face with a towel as he leaned against the side of his car and studied the final shafts of sunlight before the sun was swallowed behind the rounded hills in the west.

Wilson had learned to love the desert. He learned to love it as a boy learns to love something. But later, after his college years were over, his military service behind him, his marriage finished, he had acquired experience of things to compare it to. After he and his wife divorced in California, he returned to live in the desert and found he still loved it.

David Wilson thought he would live out the rest of his life in the desert. And die there.

He studied the gold-orange flame that spread itself over the Western horizon and after a swipe at his face with his towel he threw it onto the front seat of his car and got in and drove into old Kennewick. He parked in front of a tavern and went inside and ordered a diet soda and stood at the bar and watched the television set above the bar.

Many of the tavern customers were also watching the television, but most were waiting for the professional basketball game to come on. It was the time of year for the play-offs games to begin.

"Who's on the satellite tonight?" someone asked the bartender.

"Phoenix against Utah or Golden State and Dallas."

Wilson turned his head slightly to look at the customer who he did not recognize. Everybody knew everybody in the neighborhood tavern. "Who you betting on tonight Dave?" asked the bartender, a heavyset man about 45, the same age as Wilson. "Phoenix or Golden State."

"I'll bet a beer on Utah or Dallas, got any takers?" the stranger said looking at him.

"Thanks but I'm not drinking tonight," Wilson answered.

"Come on, you look like the sporting type, a man who knows his sports."

Wilson turned back to the television news. "Maybe."

Brandenburg Gate in Berlin came on the screen where there was a ceremony showing the removal of Checkpoint Charlie as an American military band played.

"Have you ever been to Berlin?" the stranger asked Wilson.

"Yeah, I have," Wilson answered without taking his eyes off the television set.

"How about East Berlin?"

"Nope."

"I never figured the damn thing would come down, not in my lifetime, did you?"

"Nope."

"I suppose you were in the military over there?"

"Yeah, I was."

"Interesting place isn't it?"

"Yeah, it is."

"Got any friends over there?"

"Not any more," Wilson answered, still looking at the television set.

"What kind of work do you do around here?"

"Whatever I can."

"I guess most folks around here work out on the nuclear reservation."

"I guess so."

"I heard this area got hit real hard when they had the layoffs from the shutdown of the reactors."

Wilson nodded.

"I heard they've got some real problems with cleaning up all the hot waste, some say it will take fifty years to clean it up because they say half of all the nuclear waste in the United States is buried out there. I heard the leaks were so bad that damn near anybody who lived here in the old days got poisoned."

"Where did you hear that?" David Wilson asked still looking at the television and the ceremony at Checkpoint Charlie in Berlin.

"Hell, it's in damn near every newspaper in America these days. I think anybody who reads a newspaper knows where Hanford is now. How about you, how long have you lived here?"

"A long time."

"Had any friends who got poisoned?"

Wilson finally turned to look at the man directly. "Maybe."

And he set some change on the bar and turned and left.

"Who the hell is that guy?" the stranger asked the bartender after Wilson was out the front door.

"That's David Wilson."

"Snooty type! What does he do?"

"I don't know what Dave has been doing lately, but he used to teach high school and coach sports."

"What sport did he play in college?"

"Football. David Wilson was one of the best football players to ever play around here."

The man smiled. "Sure, I remember Wilson, David Wilson."

"A lot of people don't know Dave played football, it's been a while."

"You bet I remember him. I saw him on television once when he played for the university. Wilson was a heck of a player. You never can tell who you're going to meet in a bar, can you?"

"No, sir, you never can tell, where're you from?"

"I grew up in Spokane, but I've been working for the government back in D.C. for the last twelve years."

"On vacation?"

"No, I got sent out here to write some reports."

A HOME IN BOHEMIA   7

The bartender smiled. "You're with the Department of Energy, huh?"
The man nodded. "Say, it seems to me Wilson had a brother who played football too."
"Sure. Phil. Hell'va player and he was a nice guy too."
"What happened to him?"
"After college he came back and taught school, but he got a brain tumor and died a few years ago."
"Pretty young wasn't he?"
"Yeah, pretty damn young for that. I guess David thinks he got the tumor from radiation."
"It's a mess."
The bartender seeing the news was over picked up the remote control and began searching the channels to catch the satellite signal and the basketball game.
"I didn't know about his brother," the man said to the bartender in a lower voice. Tell David Wilson the next time he comes in that I didn't know and that I'm sorry. He was a hell'va player."

David Wilson turned on his television set and went through the local stations knowing it was futile; the professional basketball game was only on the satellite. He settled on the ABC nightly news from New York and they also had a report on Checkpoint Charlie in Berlin being removed. He stared at the television picture. It seemed like a long time ago that he had been a soldier in West Germany and he had not expected the Berlin Wall to come down so suddenly.

The previous November he had watched with fascination the Berlin Wall come down. It made him think about some of his friends he had once had as a soldier there. After the Berlin Wall came down in November he watched the street marches in Prague, Czechoslovakia with the same fascination. He had studied the faces in Prague as if looking for a face of an old friend, but he had no old friends or relatives there.

Then in December the television pictures came from Bucharest and the street fighting and again David Wilson watched with fascination. When the fighting in Bucharest was over and a calm settled over Central Europe, Wilson felt a counter lull settle into his own life. It was as if he had been involved in the revolutions and the fighting though he knew he was far from the heart of either. He was, he knew, unconnected to anything so important.

The faces he had seen in the streets of Berlin, Prague and Bucharest stayed with him during the winter months and chafed against the calm, almost as if he knew or recognized some of the faces he had seen. It was as if the faces had brought alive in him the memory of some old forgotten promise he had once made.

There were no forgotten promises, no forgotten obligations to anyone, no distant relatives, no old friends to celebrate the great events with, he told himself watching the crane on television lift the guard shack of Check Point Charlie onto the bed of a military truck which would take it to a museum. His life had nothing to do with what had gone on over there and it was a long time ago that he was a soldier there and anyone who had known him must have forgotten him by now.

But a long time after the ABC news had gone to other pictures and places, David Wilson sat staring into space and not seeing anything on the television screen before him.

Chapter 2

Wilson's friendship with Father Sedlacek had begun when he was a student at St. Anthony's Grade School and continued through his college years. When Ft. Sedlacek was sent to a new parish several hours drive from Hanford, and Wilson moved out of the state with his wife, they sent each other Christmas cards.

When Ft. Sedlacek wrote Wilson in late April that he was coming to Hanford on business, Wilson wrote back immediately that he would be happy to see him.

Wilson pulled into the parking lot of the Denny's restaurant and inside found Father Sedlacek waiting by the front door. Wilson noted how the priest's complexion had turned even ruddier since they had last met and it contrasted with his hair which had turned white. They shook hands and the waitress guided them to the no smoking section. Both ordered coffee. "How long has it been, Father, since we've seen each other?" Wilson asked.

"Four or five years," Ft. Sedlacek answered with a smile.

Wilson nodded. "Time flies when you're having fun, eh?"

"So how have you been, David, you look to be in good shape?"

Wilson looked up from his coffee, a crease formed across his brow and he broke into a half-smile. "The truth is I'm a little heavy. I gained some weight this winter and I haven't been able to run it off."

Ft. Sedlacek knowing Wilson's history in athletics didn't waste a chance to needle him. "Old age is hell, huh?"

Wilson bit at his lower lip. "They say after thirty gravity takes over, I thought for a long time I'd found a way to cheat it, but the last several years it has taken its revenge all at once."

"What's bothering you David?"

Wilson's eyes lost contact with Ft. Sedlacek's and then just as quickly came back as he took a sip of coffee. "Nothing, nothing at all."

"It seems to me something has been eating at you for a long time."

Wilson tried to penetrate into Ft. Sedlacek's eyes for a clue as to what the other man was probing for, but the priest's eyes were inscrutable.

"Are you talking about Phil?"

"Maybe that's a good place to start. Have you really put it behind you or are you still letting it eat at you?"

Wilson bit at his lower lip again and looked down into his coffee cup.

"Naa, I hardly ever think about it anymore."

"Then what is it?"

"What's what?"

"What is it all about? Or haven't you noticed, David, you have been on a kind of slide for a long time?"

Wilson forced a laugh. "Slide? What are you talking about?"

Ft. Sedlacek held his smile and tried to look into Wilson's eyes but he was looked down at his coffee cup again. "You're in a slide, David. You have been sliding ever since Phil died, I think. Do you know where it will end?"

"I don't know what you're talking about, Father."

"Sure you do. I remember the first time I saw you, David. You're a teacher and you know there are certain kids you never forget because you have high hopes for them. That's the way I felt about you when I first coached you on the eighth grade football team at St. Anthony's."

Wilson nodded as he studied his coffee cup.

"You were one of the smallest runts on the team, but you fought everybody on every play no matter how big they were. Phil got the jump on you in growth, but you had more fire than Phil ever did. I remember thinking, when this little runt gets his growth he going to be real player. And I was right. You turned out to be a real player in everything you've ever done in life. So why are you sliding now, Davey, why have you turned into a quitter?"

The sound of Ft. Sedlacek calling him by his old grade school name and also calling him a quitter caught Wilson off guard. The sound quitter felt bitter to him. Wilson took a long breath. "Something changed in me after Phil died. I don't know what, it just changed and things have never felt the same since."

"When people die who we love it's right to reserve a place inside for their memory. Then we have to go on with life and make room inside for new things. We can't turn our insides into some kind of dusty museums reserved for things of the past."

"They killed him," Wilson said softly.

Ft. Sedlacek's smile was patient. "You don't know that. None of us know that."

"They killed a lot of people and then lied about it. They kept telling us there was nothing to worry about and that everything was safe. But everything was poisoned by the radiation out there. It got into the milk, into the water and into the air we breathed. And it made those rocks Phil and I used to collect out in the desert hot. I remember how Phil loved more than anything to pack a lunch and fill our canteens with water and hike out into the desert early on a Saturday morning and hunt the whole day for arrowheads and agates. They said there was nothing to worry about, but they lied to us. They killed Phil and it killed mom having to watch him die like that. Her hair went white in less than a year. I think she knew Phil was a goner from the first day they told us he had cancer. Phil tried to hide it from us, but I think he knew he was a goner too."

David Wilson paused to sip some coffee and Ft. Sedlacek kept his silence to allow him time to go on and talk it out.

"It's all crap. It's crap and it's been crap for as long as I can remember."

"Is everything crap, Davey, everything?"

"Maybe," Wilson answered.

"Does that include faith in our religion, our savior, our God?"

"Faith," Wilson repeated and looked out the restaurant window at the morning work traffic on West Kennewick Avenue. "You've asked the wrong man about faith, Father. Do you remember about five years ago you gave me a little pamphlet about the Shroud of Turin?"

"Yes, I remember it."

"You said I would find it interesting. I did. They constructed a kind of scientific argument on how the shroud must be the authentic burial cloth of Christ. It was very impressive. But it turned out their argument was false. It seems to me everything turns out that way in life. At first it seems quite the opposite, but in the end it turns out to be false. Facts always seem to get in the way. I remember in high school how our football coaches used to tell us that playing hurt would make a man out of us. I remember the old man telling me that boxing would make a man out of me and how he used to make me stand for hours at the punching bags. It would make a man out of me, he said. I remember my first football coach in college told us playing hurt would make real men out of us. It all turned out to be crap. Now one of my shoulders is no good either from football or boxing and if I tried to throw a rock across the street over there," Wilson nodded out the window. "I couldn't do it."

David Wilson took a drink of his coffee. "How long do you suppose it will be before I end up like Phil? If you breathed radiation or ate it or drank it, then it's just a question of time. And now the same people who told us there was nothing to worry about say they're going to collect data for a study and this time tell us the truth, they say. The truth is they're waiting for as many of us as possible to die because the government has no money left to pay for people like us. They lied to us for forty years and now the bill is coming due and they have no money, so it's good luck, mister, and we're sorry about it and we promise never to do it again and have a better life next time. If I'm in a slide it's because I bought into most of the nonsense without questioning it closely enough. It's sort of like this Reagan crap, this trickle down stuff. It smells like perfume if you don't get to close to it, but the people around here who lost homes probably wish they had examined it more closely. It's the same with the bureaucrats who work downtown at the school administration. They keep saying there is nothing wrong with our school system except some minor changes, but when you work inside the schools and see the product that comes out, you get sick. If we don't fix our schools we're going to be a third world country quicker than anybody thinks. Maybe we already are. And when I look around at the whole picture I see how almost everything is nothing but perfumed horse manure. I guess after Phil died I got tired of pretending about it. The same with my marriage, I finally faced the fact it took more energy to pretend it was okay than to put an end to it. I'm the wrong man to ask about faith, father."

Father Sedlacek understood by the tone of Wilson's voice it was time to begin a dialogue. He signaled to their waitress for more coffee and waited for a period of silence before he began speaking softly. "I think the time has come for you to get out of here Davey. Move on to something else. You need to say good bye to some things and put them behind you for good. You know there is an old proverb that when God closes the door to one thing he often opens a window to something else. Have you ever considered the idea that although you've lost one brother there exists the possibility that out in the world somewhere you might have someone who could be another brother to you?"

Wilson smiled politely. "No. I don't dwell on those kind of things."

"It's time for you to get out of here and put these things behind you."

"I like it here. I've tried living in other places and I like it here better than any place I've ever been."

"All right, you like the desert. But you're in a slide and do you know where that ends?"

Wilson looked back out the window. "I don't care where it ends."

"It ends up in being a derelict. Have you ever seen how a derelict ends up?"

"Have you forgotten I used to lived with one."

"Your father wasn't a derelict, Davey. He had a drinking problem but for a long time he put a roof over your head and was a good man doing his duty as a father. And we don't know how he ended up."

"That smells a little too much like perfume to me and I think we both know how he ended up even if we don't know when or where."

Father Sedlacek smiled. "Davey, you've always been a fighter and you've got to get involved with life again. So you've got to get out of here and leave this behind you. I know of a situation I think is just right for you and you're the perfect man for the job."

Wilson glanced into Ft. Sedlacek's eyes and felt the priest's warmth penetrate into him so he couldn't help smiling in return. He shook his head from side to side. "Okay, let's hear it."

"I have a distant relative in Czechoslovakia and he is a director of a high school there and he needs an English teacher."

Wilson's eyebrows lifted. "You're serious aren't you?"

"Of course I am. It's perfect for you. The moment I got his letter I thought of you. Believe me this would change your life."

"I'm sure of that, but if I wanted to change my life that bad why not find a situation in Russia? I mean why not just go right to the bottom and get it over with, why stop in Czechoslovakia?"

Ft. Sedlacek's smile deepened as if he had not heard the sarcasm in Wilson's remark. "They're trying to build a new country, Davey. Can you imagine the excitement of building a new country sort of like our pioneers felt when they came out here. Most of these people have never known freedom. And I'm sure they need some athletic coaches and teachers and - "

"And you want me to teach them how to be real men!"

Ft. Sedlacek once again ignored the sarcasm and continued on in an enthusiastic voice. "They want to learn English and they want to build new lives where their children can have something decent and good, like we have here. They need people to teach them who have the spirit and the guts and determination from experience. That's you, Davey. The first time I saw you get your face pushed in the mud by some kid twenty pounds bigger than you and saw that you were the first kid to be back on his feet ready to go again, I felt there was something special about you and I always hoped there was a special place and a special job for you in this world. Well, this is it. They need a man like you."

Wilson laughed politely. "I can't imagine them needing a man like me because I'd tell them about things that happened here, things like Hanford."

"Sure tell them. They need to hear things aren't perfect here and that we've made mistakes too. Tell them we have the same kind of bad apples in our country and in our past as they do. But let them see what a good apple looks like that was produced here in our culture and in our soil. Let them see what a good apple looks like up close."

David Wilson ran his fingers through his hair and fingered the side of his jaw.

"The name of this game is life, Davey, and here is a chance for you to start over and get involved again. Don't miss it."

Wilson laughed, but softly. "So I was the first guy you thought of, huh? You want to send some old wreck to some place where they probably already have too many old wrecks. What they need is some young blood, like some of these Reaganites who believe in trickle down economics and don't worry be happy stuff. Not some old blood like me."

Ft. Sedlacek cuffed Wilson on a shoulder. "Oh, we're too old for that stuff, they need to know just the opposite. They need to know that life even here is full of troubles but that men overcome them. Sometimes a man overcomes his own troubles by getting involved with people and helping them. Once you get a taste of really helping people your slide will end. But you've got to want to do it as bad as you wanted to be good in football, for example. Life is like football in that respect; everything really boils down to how bad a man wants to do something. Believe me, this is a chance for you to start something new and good and leave something worn out and harmful behind you."

"I don't know a thing about Czechoslovakia except that they've been living for a long time under communists, since the end of the war, I guess."

"It's not important how much you know, I've brought this book along for you to look through." Quickly without losing his smile he lifted several books out of his briefcase and set them on the table before Wilson. "Go on, take them home with you. Look them over."

"What's the point of it, even if I wanted to go I don't have enough spare bucks to get from here to anywhere. Substitute teachers live from payday to payday. So what's the point of it?"

Ft. Sedlacek's smile deepened and his eyes warmed. "Oh, don't argue about details, Davey. The ways of the Lord are mysterious. Just take these books home and look them over and I'll be in touch with you."

"What's the name of the place where your relative lives?"

"Pilsen, a city in Western Czechoslovakia, the part known as Bohemia."

"They make beer there, don't they?"

"Yes indeed, some people say it's the best beer in the world."

Wilson sat looking at the books without speaking or touching them, as if to acknowledge them would set in motion some chain of events he could not reverse. At last he bit his lower lip. "Sure, why not. It doesn't hurt to look at a couple of books."

He turned to Ft. Sedlacek. "But it doesn't mean I think this is a good idea or approve of it. I'll just look at the books."

"Take a good look, Davey. Did you see any of the television coverage of the revolution last November in Prague?"

"Yeah, I watched it all. It was interesting."

"Did you see the happiness in some of those faces, they're poor but happy and proud and they want a chance to build something new and good. You can be a part of that, Davey. I wish I could go myself. Do you know what the best feeling in the world is? I mean the feeling that nothing else come close to? It's knowing you've built something good enough that it's going to be around even after you're gone from this old world. That's when you feel real life in your veins, anything else is just imitation life."

David Wilson glanced into Ft. Sedlacek's eyes and nodded his head ever so slightly as if he understood and agreed.

Chapter 3

The first Saturday following Father Sedlacek's visit was the first warm day of the new spring. The sun rose in a cloudless sky over the desert turning the rounded hills in the west a warm brown color. David Wilson was up early, as always, and as he walked to his car he felt the change in the morning air. It was going to be hot in the afternoon.

He drove to a McDonald's restaurant and, as usual, was one of the first customers. Often he was the first customer. He ordered a cup of coffee and lifted the *Spokane Review* newspaper from the courtesy rack. The Review wasn't much of a newspaper and in some ways even less reading than the local paper, *The Tri-City Herald,* but the habit of reading a newspaper with his first cup of morning coffee had taken root so long ago that it was cemented in his daily routine.

On Saturday mornings Wilson would stop at a shop and buy a Seattle newspaper, the *Post-Intelligencer,* to read in addition to the Spokane paper. That Saturday morning he read his newspapers and drank two cups of coffee and drove four miles to the west where there was an open stretch of land situated between a housing development and shopping centers on the other sides. In the middle of the sage carpeted land was a small city airport where Wilson liked to do his jogging more than any other place. The sprawling tract of land was an island of tranquility which was located in an area called the Highlands. From the promontory of the Highlands Wilson could see in every direction the vastness of the desert and the hills. To the north across the river were farm lands which looked like colored patches of a quilt, to the northwest were the white domes of the nuclear reactors and due west were the string of humpbacked hills known as the Rattlesnake Mountains.

It had been that way for thousands of years, Wilson often thought as he ran in late afternoon with the sun setting behind the hills, but the nuclear reactors changed everything for even more thousands of years. The hot nuclear waste buried in the desert would make it forbidden territory for as long as anyone could imagine. It was in complete contrast to what the original Indians loved the land for. The natives made their home there because of the mild winters, the plentiful fish in the river, the wild birds and wild fruits and vegetables which grew in the volcanic soil. Life had been so good for the them in the desert of Hanford that they came to feel it was a place favored by God and had religious ceremonial grounds where the plutonium was eventually made for the world's first atomic bomb.

David Wilson had not thought out a position on what God favored in life or on earth or even if he believed in God, still when he jogged through the solitude of the sage covered island surrounded on all sides by advancing buildings, he found a tranquility settle in him so that his mood became calm.

But that Saturday morning a discontent ate at him and the bite of it wouldn't release itself as he jogged under a sunny sky. Back in the McDonald's restaurant he had read a story in one of the morning newspapers that kept returning in his mind as he ran.

"East Germany's former Stalinist regime secretly
 guillotined 62 political prisoners and burned
 their bodies in the 1950s, according to the state
 crematorium director in Dresden."

That was it. There were no other details. It was such a tiny story that it was almost lost on the page. But it sprang off the page at Wilson and wouldn't leave him.

David Wilson had studied history in college. So he was not

ignorant of the fact that after World War II there were countless crimes against innocent persons and violations of human rights in the countries where communists took over control. In one of the ironies of modern history, even before the Nurnburg trials were over and the executions of Nazis carried out, crimes just as brutal and ruthless were being committed by communists. Wilson never felt moved to learn the details, to the contrary he felt a need to avoid learning the details of that history. It was a kind of escapism, he once conceded to himself years after he had gradu- ated from college, for just as with the radiation contamination from the Hanford project, there seemed a kind of futility in learning that history as it linked modern history and modern man together in a way that suggested something repugnant.

Wilson struggled to the end of his run, a four mile course. During the run an image of a guillotine kept popping into his mind at unexpected moments and at other moments he saw men being led to the guillotine and their murder. Despite the brilliant weather he did not feel relaxed by the run, something inside him felt congested and heavy.

"It was unlucky to live in places like East Germany or Russia or Czechoslovakia or any other places where communists took over," he thought as he walked over the asphalt of a parking lot to cool off. "But it was also unlucky to live near Hanford when the radiation had secretly spilled out over the countryside contamina- ing everything in its path. Everything in life, it seemed, was a matter of being in the right place at the time - or of not being in the wrong place at the wrong time."

As he walked, Wilson entered into a familiar argument with himself, could a man, any man, really change anything for the better in today's world? They said some of the hot waste material buried out in the desert would stay hot for about 50,000 years, give or take a few thousand years. It seemed to Wilson something unchangeable had been set in motion by someone in Washington, D.C. just as a decision was made about Czechoslovakia in Washington, D.C. about the same time. Individual lives were changed by those decisions and the fate of people weren't factored into the process by bureaucrats. People were numbers like so many acres or hectares of timber or wheat and they made policies for people no matter whether they were Americans living in the desert at Hanford or farmers living in Bohemia. That was the reality of modern life. That's the way it was, brother, and you couldn't change it.

Wilson removed his baseball cap and with the back of his hand cleared his forehead of sweat. How could a man like Father Sedlacek actually believe one man could make any difference in anything? In fact, how could an intelligent and strong man like Sedlacek believe in religion? They said that when he played football in the 1940s at Gonzaga he was so good and so tough that he was feared by other players. No question, Sedlacek was a real man.

Wilson had walked in a circle around the parking lot and had arrived back at where his car was parked. He removed his towel from the front seat and sat down on the car's front bumper and studied the desert landscape as he had countless times before. He thought once again how the sky over the desert was the purest blue he had seen anywhere. The idea of moving away and living anywhere else, especially a place as distant as Czechoslovakia, seemed to him absurd. Still, there was some truth in Ft. Sedlacek's words that he couldn't run away from: he was in a slide, perhaps not a dramatic one that was obvious to someone who didn't know him. He was able to pay his bills, so long as he avoided anything like a major medical bill, and he was solvent.

But a closer look at his life as seen through the eyes of someone who had known him for as long as Ft. Sedlacek would be more revealing. It would reveal flaws in the fabric of his life that where not seen by strangers. It would reveal he had cut himself off from old friends and hadn't bothered to make new ones. Wilson mopped up the sweat that had build up again across his forehead

22 A HOME IN BOHEMIA

with his towel and nodded to himself, as if to acknowledge something Ft. Sedlacek had said. Yes, sir, Sedlacek had hit a bulls eye: he was in a kind of slide and had been in one for a long time. But a derelict! He was sure wrong there.

Derelicts are those wine heads along First Avenue in Seattle who panhandle for their next bottle of bad wine. How could he possibly ever end up like that? Could it start by something like having a major medical bill he couldn't pay? Wilson had read stories of homeless people who had done nothing more than get sick and not have the medical insurance to cover their bills and then losing their home. Was he on a collision course with such an ending that would place him on First Avenue or sleeping in his car?

He had in a sense opted out of the system by failing to look for a full time teaching position after he was laid off when the school district lost enrollment when some of the reactors were shut down by the government. Instead of moving away to find another teaching position he opted to stay behind and accept substitute teaching. It left him without benefits such as health insurance and vulnerable to financial disaster if he ever became ill or had a serious accident.

But he found there was a satisfaction in no longer having to stuff his briefcase full of papers to grade at home, to no longer have to fill out weekly lesson plans on school forms - plans that nobody read and teachers seldom if ever followed. To no longer have to sit through the ritual Monday afternoon meetings in which teachers labored to keep some sort of intelligent look on their faces while some gas bag from the district office read meaningless reports and then asked for comments, which only the most vapid souls could possibly have an intelligent comment. If the same wind bag had gotten up and read a report on the annual rainfall on some plateau on the moon, it would have made nod difference. The same teachers would have labored to keep intelligent expressions plastered on their faces and the same ones would have made the same asinine comments about how the district report mirrored their own opinion.

Thinking back to those meetings on Monday afternoons Wilson smiled and thought maybe going to a place such as Czechoslovakia wasn't so absurd or at least no more absurd than his present life. Father Sedlacek said he would only have to make a one-year commitment, what could be so terrible about that? And Father Sedlacek promised to arrange for his air fair over. So what had he really to lose except one year of his life?

And children in Czechoslovakia couldn't be any more outrageous, stupid, rude, and lazy than the American kids Wilson had seen coming through the pipeline. Year by year he had noticed how the behavior of his students became worse until rules in most schools became ignored not merely by the students but also by the teachers because they knew they would not be enforced by the administration. Policies were made by the bureaucrats in the district offices to cover groups and the idea of individual responsibility vanished. At election time school boards hauled out old slogans about returning to the "old values that made our country and schools the best in the world." But nobody believed it anymore and hadn't for a long time, least of all the teachers.

And each year Wilson noticed that the better teachers opted out of the system, if they could find another job, because they had lost all their patience and hope. So what had he really to lose by going to a place called Pilsen? If you've opted out of the system you might as well go to Bohemia!

Wilson stood up and put his weight gingerly on his right knee, the knee he had hurt playing football. It sometimes stiffened up after a run.

The truth was, he admitted as he took a deep breath, he had little to lose by going to a place called Czechoslovakia. Once you were exposed to the radiation from Hanford there was only one outcome, wasn't there? It was inevitable, wasn't it? It was only a question of time. And nobody could change it.

Chapter 4

It was dark and five in the morning when Wilson lugged his baggage off his train into the Plzen Central Station. He couldn't read any of the signs and he stood in the chill of the morning trying to figure out which way to go. Inside the old station it was dark and dirty feeling, half-hiding two large statues dedicated to working socialist men and women. A sour smell drifted throughout the main hall telling Wilson somewhere near was a latrine with bad plumbing. Welcome home, brother, Wilson whispered to himself and allowed himself a smile.

plumbing. Welcome home, brother, Wilson whispered to himself and allowed himself a smile.

Finally he spotted a sign over two swinging doors, *Samoobsluha,* and a light from behind the glass windows of the doors made him move toward what he hoped was a canteen with hot coffee. Behind the doors he found a dimly lit cafeteria-style snack bar. He stacked his baggage at the foot of the first empty table and made a sweep of the room. It had the same grimy feel of the main station and the customers wore the faces of refugees from the last tavern to close. A few were drinking coffee but most were drinking from mugs of beer. Wilson walked past the waiter drawing beer to a tired looking woman at the cash register and ordered coffee in German.

Stirring sugar into his muddy coffee, thick with floating grounds, Wilson took time to inspect the unshaven faces of men dressed in shabby clothing and began trying to absorb the language that was not only unfathomable to him but alien to his ears. The longer he sat in the *Samoobsluha* and absorbed the strange sounds around him the more intense became the feeling that he had entered a world that was different than anything he imagined. The feeling was strong enough that he felt like he had penetrated a fog bank so fine that only the inner senses could sense the change he had entered, but the outer senses couldn't feel it.

He nursed a second cup of the strong coffee waiting for daylight and then hefted his backpack and duffle bag and the box of books by the belt around he fashioned from a military web belt and left the room. He found a place in the ground floor of the station to secure his baggage and went outside for his first look at Plzen.

His first look came around the corner from the station on Moskevska Street and he saw old buildings coated with what looked like years of accumulated coal dust, soot, dirt, gasoline exhaust and faded paint. Broken plaster revealed bricks that were blackened and chipped. The sidewalks were poured unevenly creating pools of water to collect in places, in other places the windows boarded over.

The morning auto traffic on Moskevska Street was light and the cars ran over a cobblestone fashioned from a stone face rougher and larger than regular brick face creating a loud hum from the tires and a thumping sound. Wilson looked at the cars with a curiosity. They were almost all small and bore the scars of fenders and doors amputated from other cars to create a kind of mutation that he had seen only in American poverty belts such as the slums of large cities.

The electric trolley busses and street cars fit into a scheme: like the buildings, they were aged and covered with soot and grime. The faces Wilson met on the street fit into another scheme: they would not make eye contact or smile. And the pedestrians he passed on Moskevska Street were dressed as if a law had been made outlawing any bright colors such as yellow or orange or green or even sky blue. Taken as a whole, the dark old train station, decayed old buildings, mutated automobiles, gloomily dressed and poker-faced pedestrians, the picture Wilson received was of gloom.

He tried to resist the blade of the gloom as it cut, but he could not. The collected mass of greys and blacks overcame him as easily as acid breaks through a coat of paint to protect metal from rust.

When he found the city block his school sat on, his spirit rebounded. He found a proud old building with a high columned portico over the front entrance giving it a Greek flavor. There were statues at each end of the portico then he discovered it was not his building. His school was on the back side of the block. Walking around the block he found his school had the same coating of soot and black as the other buildings of Plzen. It did, however, have a clean looking red roof that was bright in the morning sunshine. Wilson smiled. "Welcome home, brother."

Looking across the street from his school he saw the fronts of several old buildings with frescoes painted on them that was a contrast to the dark and the grime of the other building fronts. And further up the street he saw several apartment buildings with statues sculptured into the spaces which divided one apartment unit from the other. One statue was a duplicate of Venus. It brought a smile out of Wilson. The old Bohemian city, despite its decay, must have once breathed charm into the lives who lived in it. Biting his lower lip Wilson considered that perhaps the ghosts of the past still hovered over Plzen. A half century of neglect darkened everything until it groaned and cried for attention, but even after a half century of neglect some of the old buildings with their frescoes and statues sang a song that breathed something sweet into the air that neither the communists nor the pollution could silence.

Wilson turned his back on Venus and took the front steps of the school two at a time. Wilson was fueled by the challenge he felt. It was what he had thrived on all his life - challenge.

Chapter 5

After meeting Father Sedlacek's relative, several teachers and receiving a tour of the old school building, Wilson was left alone in his new office, a narrow cubicle with four desks in it. One of the doors opened up to the backside of his classroom, number 16. He got up from his desk and opened the door and walked to the front of his new classroom and sat on top of the desk.

The insides of the old building had a smell Wilson remembered from his youth when he attended a grade school with wooden floors that had been refinished, waxed, and buffed so many times for so many years that the floors had a sweet smell of mixed oils as a broom closet smells where waxes, oils and cleaning rags are stored together.

The smell brought to life pleasant memories such as the memory of the face of his kindergarten teacher, Mrs. Kimble. His kindergarten had the same old light globes hung from the ceiling that hung from his new classroom. Thinking of Mrs. Kimble after so many years made Wilson reflect on how some faces never completely left a man no matter how many years passed.

He stood up, arms still folded across his chest, as if he was going to deliver a lecture to a room full of students, and looked out over the rows of empty desks covered in places by shadows and in other places bathed in blocks of brilliant sunshine that came through the windows. On the first day of every new school year he reconciled himself to the idea some student would innocently sit before him, never suspecting their face would lodge forever in his memory like a sphinx. It happened with regularity year after year. It was not always a pretty or handsome face. It must be, he'd speculated, every face has some kind of message encoded into it and that messages registered on the subconscious. He wondered if it could be that every person brings some past experience, perhaps something stamped in their genes, that found its way into the face and one could never be safe from receiving that encoded message no matter whether it was good or bad, pleasing or unpleasant. If true then it meant a man was always vulnerable to faces. Wilson stood with his arms folded across his chest and continued to look at the rows of empty desks, as if hoping to find an answer to an old riddle that had eluded him for so many years in the silent desks and chairs. His jaw muscles flexed.

Wilson's memory returned to an old face that for year brought him discomfort. It was a pretty face. He met her one summer working in a restaurant as a waitress. It was the year after his divorce. She was slender and dark-haired and whenever he would come into the restaurant she would smile warmly at him. Their conversations were always polite as it was obvious she was too young a woman for him to become involved with romantically. He could easily have been her father, Wilson speculated. Then one afternoon she invited him to meet her after work and Wilson agreed. Seeing her out of her work uniform in jeans and a sleeveless summer shirt, her dark hair falling almost to her shoulders, he saw her for the first time as a woman without considering how old she was. At that meeting something sprang to life in him. Something uncontrolled and with a life of its own. He felt threatened and confused by the new feeling and all the feelings were increased when he learned she was a high school student, a senior. It brought something alive inside him close to terror. He resolved to hide his feelings so that no one could ever guess the depths of his confusion.

After the end of the summer and the beginning of the new school year his resolve gave way to depression because his feelings didn't weaken but deepened. Complicating things was the sense he had that she saw his confusion; when he visited the restaurant there was no longer a friendly smile from her but the smile of a woman who shared something unspoken with a man deeper that of friendship. Wilson felt a challenge in her smile, but it terrorized him all the more. He willed himself against it the same way he did when he had trained to play football or another sport in his school days. But even as he did so he sensed it was doomed to fail because this struggle was on a level that involved a man's spiritual life.

Mary Kennedy was literate and intelligent and sent him letters which he studied word by word, sentence by sentence trying to probe behind words into the secret by ways of her mind. He found himself compelled to answer her letters and their relationship evolved onto another plane. He found himself avoiding her restaurant except when he noticed her car was not there. He also began to fear being called to substitute teach at her school, afraid he might meet her in the hall or worse have her sit in one of his classes for an hour.

By the arrival of winter Wilson felt stuck in the bottom of a dark pit. For the first time in his life he was trapped in depression. And for the first time he found himself sometimes unable to sleep. On one such sleepless night wrestling with Mary Kennedy he found a thought that seemed to free him and also confuse him: Mary Kennedy bore a striking likeness to a woman he had once known before his marriage. Pat.

He met Pat the first year he was out of the Army in Portland, Oregon. After the first phase of their relationships she often brought up the subject of commitment which Wilson felt was a kind of code word for marriage. Wilson had no desire for marriage with her or anyone else at that time. It lead to friction and then arguments and finally to separation. Their final argument brought bitter words from Pat, she accused him of being selfish and insincere and wanting the pleasures of marriage without accepting the obligations. Her words were razor sharp and cut Wilson, though he pretended the opposite.

After the breakup Wilson was surprised how deeply he missed Pat. He tried to remove the sting by dating new women, but it was a failure. After several weeks he decided to attempt a reconciliation, but he found she had moved out of her apartment without leaving a forwarding address. At her office he learned she had quit her job. Once gain Wilson feinted indifference and told himself his discomfort was only a passing tide. Other women filled in the gaps of his life until he married, but the memory of Pat never quite washed itself out on the tides of other relationships, not even his marriage. There came unexpected moments when her memory stood before him. He always dismissed such moments as attacks of nostalgia for his bachelor days.

But after his divorce he learned of Pat's death - a suicide. For several weeks he felt a sensation that brought alive the old discomfort and emptiness. It was a year later that he met Mary Kennedy. She was an similar in many ways to Pat not only in her face, but the way she spoke, the way she was built, even in the way she walked.

It was then for the first time Wilson understood the meaning of vulnerability to things undefined which went beyond logic or understanding. There were things that really did seem to have a life of their own and which couldn't be resisted by setting one's will against them. For a man one of those things was a woman's face or even voice which could bring alive an old memory long after he assumed it to be dead. Some things simply never died, Wilson marveled in resignation. They would follow a man to the end of his days.

David Wilson unfolded his arms to let them come to rest against his sides in a posture that seemed to be resignation. He took note of the fact there was a single picture hung in the room, an official looking black and white photograph of Vaclav Havel hung above one corner of the front blackboard. He resolved to find some pictures to hang and brighten up the austere feel of the room. He brought his hands together forcefully as a football or basketball coach does before sending his team out to face an opposing team and strode out of his new classroom.

Chapter 6

Wilson was given an apartment located in a government housing complex where square grey buildings rose uniformly over the landscape to a height of seven stories. It had two small rooms plus a bathroom. The toilet didn't work, the kitchen sink's pipes leaked a stream of water over the counter when turned on, the washing machine was out of order and the school offered to supply a refrigerator and old black and white television set. The toilet would be repaired directly, he was promised, so it wouldn't leak over the floor.

"Welcome home, brother," Wilson whispered to himself and smiled at first sight of his new apartment. As the day gave way to evening and street lights of the city began lining the darkness, he stood looking out his kitchen window from the sixth floor, he wished he had thought to bring along a beer or two to celebrate his new home.

His classes were roughly the same size as they were in America and most of the faces of his students could have blended in easily with the faces of his American students. When he first saw the list of names of his students he sighed at the names he could not pronounce and which provoked laughter when he tried to say them in class.

He was surprised by how much English some of his students knew and how much they knew about the United States. And after several weeks Wilson fell into much the same kind of routine he was used to in an American school, except that his classes were easier to teach as the behavior of Czech students was more polite and orderly than he was used to in America.

One exception of his routine was because the school had no cafeteria he had to buy his lunches in a government canteen in the basement of a building a block from the school. He was told by Jane Tozantova, an English teacher whose desk was next to his, with a smile that the canteen until the revolution was strictly for communist party officials. Most of them, she added, were still there, though the mood was a bit subdued since the revolution. Wilson smiled, he had never eaten with communists. "Welcome home brother," he whispered under his breath.

"Excuse me," Jane said.
"Oh nothing. Just a saying we have."
"Welcome home, brother? You can't be a communist?"
"No, of course not," Wilson laughed. "It only means there is a first time for everything, sort of."
"Oh, you'll enjoy them. They're a cheerful bunch."
"I'll bet. How is the food?"
"Like you would expect in a canteen."
"Hot with lots of gravy."
"Yes, I hope you're fond of gravy."
Wilson smiled. "I survived Army food."
Jane Tozantova smiled without comment.
"Is it that bad?" Wilson asked.
"It's typical Czech food. Lots of dumplings, lots of gravy, a little meat and hardly ever any green vegetables. But it's hot."
"And cheap," Wilson said calculating that the hundred odd *korun* he paid for a two week lunch ticket cost about five dollars.
"Oh a man telephoned this morning and wants to talk to you about coaching a boy's basketball team. His name and telephone number are on the note I left on your desk."
Wilson scanned his desk and picked up a piece of paper. "How did he get my name? I'm not a basketball coach."
"Oh, you've been here one week and I'm sure your name is well-known by now outside the school. And you look like the sort of chap who has played sports, so I volunteered your name."

Wilson looked at his colleague who not only talked with a British accent but had a dry way of needling a person that the English use. He understood at that moment his colleague understood far more about him that he did about her. Having visited England as a student, then marrying an Englishman, she had somehow bridged the gap between a language and its humor.

"Thanks. Is there anything else you've volunteered me for that I should know about?"

"Not yet," she replied with a smile.

"But I'm not a basketball coach. I was once a football coach, but American football and that's nothing like basketball."

"Oh, you can do it. The boys are counting on you."

"What do you mean?"

"They don't like their present coach. He's a buffoon. And surely you've played basketball before?"

"Yes, of course. I played in high school, about thirty years ago. I did a lot of things thirty years ago, but I can't do some of them now."

"You'll love the boys."

"How do you know?"

"I know one of them. He used to be a neighbor of mine. He's a lovely boy and as time passes you'll need something to break up the time. Go ahead and call the man and go visit him. There is a game Saturday morning, I'll go with you."

Wilson looked at her and nodded. "Sure."

"You'll love it David."

"They're probably a bunch of midgets and haven't won a game in years."

"That's a poor attitude to have before you ever see them."

Wilson smiled. "I did coach a basketball team once. It was my first year of teaching. The regular coach got sick and was out for the year, so they asked me to coach them. I said yes before I'd really thought about it. Being my first year of teaching I wanted to be helpful, but it was the most miserable year of teaching I ever had. It was in a small town and there was barely enough boys to make a squad."

Wilson stopped and laughed. "Those boys weren't much good at football because they were slow and only of average size. But in basketball when you are one step slow it is a huge advantage for the opponent and if you are two steps slow, then it is murder and if you are short and slow it is absolute murder. Those boys were slow and short and they were also slow thinkers. The first time I saw them practice I thought, we won't win a single game, I don't care how bad the other team is. And we didn't win a single game. I now know why the regular coach was sick. I've wondered since then if in some small towns out in the countryside if there isn't a lot of incest or something because all those boys had similar characteristics and the odds would seem to work against so many boys of the same age having those kind of negative traits. I hate losing and that season seemed to go on forever. I promised myself when the school year was over I was leaving that town because I couldn't stand the idea of seeing any of those boys again. But the lesson I learned is never to volunteer for anything until you see the situation in the flesh. How old are these boys?"

"Sixteen through eighteen. They're called junior boys."

"How about the boy you know?"

"His name is Robert and he is sixteen or seventeen. His mother is a basketball trainer and he has been playing for six or seven years. He is really quite good and speaks some English."

"But he's short, right?"

"No he's not short and he's not tall."

"I didn't know anybody played basketball here, I thought Czechs only played tennis and soccer."

"Oh no. Czechs play many sports besides tennis and soccer. We play ice hockey too, but it's true we don't play much basketball. We play volleyball, in fact, a group of teachers play every Wednesday after school down in the basement gym. You ought to come down and join us this week."

"Volleyball! I haven't played basketball for at least ten years, but I can't even remember the last time I played volleyball. I don't like it, it doesn't seem like a real sport to me."

"Oh, come on, Wilson. The other teachers want to have a look at you."

"I know I'll be sorry, but for you I'll do it. But just once. Because I really do hate volleyball."

"You're not serious?"

"I am serious. If you can't bump someone then it isn't a real sport."

Jane Tozantova looked perplexed.

"In a real sport you're allowed to bump, to push, to wear the other guy down. If you can't touch them then it's not a real sport."

"You mean like your American football where people are running into each other."

"Yes, exactly."

"But it's so primitive, Wilson. There is no grace or tactics to it."

"Sure there are, if you understand it. And even in basketball you're allowed to nudge a fellow or bump him or give him a hip when you're going for a rebound."

"Give him a hip?"

Wilson stood up and assumed a position of a basketball player bent at the knees and arms extended. "Sure. We call it clearing out. Look when the other team misses a shot you've got to establish your spot under the basket. Naturally the guy with the best spot gets the ball. So you've got to use your butt or backside as a lever to move the other guy."

Wilson illustrated his technique by blocking out a file cabinet with a bump from his hips and then a shoulder. The file cabinet gave out a groan before coming to a stop.

She stared at Wilson. "I say, you're rather keen on that kind of thing, aren't you?"

Wilson's smile revealed his satisfaction. "Yes, I'm rather keen on it."

"Sort of primitive, aren't you?"

"Primitive?"

"Yes, you seem to know a lot about books and history, but I think you're rather primitive just beneath the surface, Wilson."

"You don't mean primitive like a Russian, do you?"

"No."

"What do you mean?"

"I mean I think there is something rebellious about you that you can't control."

Wilson laughed.

"No I'm quit sure of it," Jane Tozantova insisted.

Wilson studied her to see if she was merely needling him in her fashion, but he couldn't measure her intent.

"I suppose we're all rather rebellious at one time of another, aren't we?"

"No most Czechs have learned not to be. Most have learned the art of merely going along with whomever happens to be in control at the moment. They've learned not to voice their true feelings, except at home. After fifty years of being ruled by outsiders they've learned the art of surviving and not taking chances."

"Well I enjoy some bumping and pushing in sports. I always have. And I hate losing."

Jane smiled. "You're going to have to learn some patience to live successfully in Czechoslovakia, Wilson."

Wilson already had his first lesson in patience. It took his toilet two weeks to get fixed and the kitchen faucet still leaked. And there was no hope for the washing machine. He had accepted the idea of doing his laundry by hand in his miniature bathtub.

Chapter 7

The basketball team was about what Wilson expected - it was what he feared. On a clear Saturday morning he went with Jane Tozantova to the gym to watch them play a team from a town called Nymburk. Lokomotiva Boys Junior Basketball team was neither tall nor quick, neither did they play with intelligence or guile. They managed a comfortable lead and let it slip away during the second half and lost by a basket in the final seconds. It brought their coach off his chair in a rage, directed at one player in particular who had made a stupid error that sent the opponent to the foul line. He was the tallest of the Lokomotiva boys and the lanky boy began yelling in return at the coach. It seemed to Wilson a kind of comedy.

But Jane's former neighbor, Robert, was a surprise: he could play basketball. He was spindly and frail looking and his face looked to be that of a boy closer to fourteen than sixteen. He was of average height, but what caught Wilson's attention was that he played hard and fearlessly challenged larger players around the basket. But on defense he seemed like all the other Lokomotiva players: timid and indifferent. Looking at Robert, Wilson thought that in a year or two, if he grew a couple of inches and put on some weight, he could be a real player. Maybe even good enough to sign up with a college or university in the States.

Robert looked up to where they were sitting and smiled at them and Wilson smiled politely in return.

"Well?" Jane asked.

"They don't know how to play basketball."

"I told you their coach is a buffoon, you could see for yourself how he screams at the players."

"They're the kind of boys which could drive any coach crazy and even if he was a genius he couldn't make them taller or more intelligent."

"It's a challenge isn't it, Wilson?"

He glanced at her. "I know what you're up to."

"You're the kind of chap who loves a challenge. Shall I tell them you accept?"

"What do I need with indigestion? This team isn't a challenge, it's instant heartburn."

"You're tough, Wilson. And primitive. You're not afraid of a little heartburn. You're the rugged American from the wild west, you're not supposed to be afraid of anything."

Wilson smiled weakly. "I'm afraid of lots of things including slow and short basketball teams. Believe me, I'm afraid of lots of things."

"They need a chap like you, you can see that."

"They don't need me, they need a kind of miracle man to bless them with fast feet and glands to make them taller and smarter."

Robert had showered and approached them where they sat in the empty stands. He stood before them smiling and looking nervous. "I am sorry we played very badly today."

Wilson nodded and shook his hand. Up close he seemed even younger. "Never mind. Every player and every team has their bad days."

"You will be our new trainer?"

Wilson shot a glance at Jane. "Well, I haven't decided yet."

"Everybody says they want you to be our trainer."

"I haven't coached a basketball team for a long time."

Wilson felt the boy's eyes weigh on him. He could see the hope in his eyes. "How many boys on the team can understand some English?"

"Just me and one other boy."

"How many can understand German?"

"Three maybe four."

Wilson's eyes narrowed and he looked at Jane as if to say, see what did I tell you, it's impossible. "I know basketball," Wilson began speaking slowly. "I played it when I was about your age for a man who knew basketball as well as anyone can know it. His system was very simple, but precise and demanding. A player had to learn certain habits that cannot be learned quickly. They look simple but require discipline. I don't know if I can help you and your team. I would like to, believe me, I would like to. But I don't know if I can."

"We will learn your system," Robert answered cheerfully.

Wilson ran a hand over his chin. "No, it's not that easy."

"We will learn it," Robert insisted.

Wilson smiled. "How many years have you been playing basketball?"

"Seven years."

"You're very good at dribbling the ball."

"I love it and practice every day."

Wilson nodded his approval. "If you're going to play basketball, then you had better love it."

"Do you love basketball?"

"Oh, I guess I did once when I was your age."

"Where is your home in America?"

"In a place you've never heard of. It's out in the Western desert."

"I hope you will become our trainer, Mr. Wilson," Robert said holding out his hand.

"He is a very nice boy and intelligent too, I think," Wilson remarked to Jane as they walked toward a bus stop.

"His mother and father are divorced. His mother, the basketball trainer, is the one who got Robert interested in it. It's a terrible thing for a boy his age not to have a father at home."

"I know," Wilson said looking up toward the sky over Plzen.

"You'll coach them, of course?"

Wilson's voice lowered. "Perhaps you thought I was exaggerating when I told Robert I once played for a coach who knew basketball as well as anyone. But it's true. He was just a man in a small town out in the desert. We never thought much about him as boys because when you are that young you never think too much about the shape of things. I mean you simply accept the adult world as it is. Before the second world war the town didn't exist and our town wasn't pretty because everything in it was built and owned by the government and everything looked like military buildings. But as boys we didn't care and we liked our town. The basketball gym we played in was modern for the time and we thought it was a wonderful gym because we had such a good coach and won almost all our games every years. It made us feel proud. So people filled up our gym for our games and were also proud of us. It was those kind of memories that made living there seem special after we had grown up. Even our weather seemed better than anywhere else we knew of, we didn't have the rain the bigger cities had near the ocean and we didn't have the bitter winters of the places just beyond the desert in the other direction. Even in winter we often had sunshine and mild days. And we thought our girls were prettier than those from the towns and cities nearby, as if our sunshine and dry weather somehow made them prettier as it sweetened the local grapes. Every year in March they had the big basketball tournament in Seattle and we won a place in the tournament almost every year, but we never won it. Without speaking about it I think we all believed the city boys were smarter than us and it was only natural we should lose to them. Then in my junior year we won the championship in Seattle. I was sixteen and to me it seemed the grandest thing I could imagine. I still remember the night and how for just an instant I wished time would stop and I could have it forever. Even at sixteen I think you can recognize special moments that will never come again and you try to catch them and hold onto them. The next year our coach had some problem with his heart and his assistant took over. He knew the system but it wasn't the same as the year before. I graduated and left our town as did most of the other boys on the team. Now when I see a photograph of our team celebrating that night in the locker room, that's still on display in the trophy case in the school, it seems very strange, as if it was only a dream."

Wilson stopped talking as they walked and bit his lower lip out of habit. "I learned that man's system and maybe to boys who spoke English I could teach some of the basics over several years. It's not that complicated, no more complicated than learning some dances, but this dance must be in perfect rhythm with four other people. Some people can learn to think like that and some never can, it's their personality not intelligence or physical skill that stops them. In my memory it is something close to perfect because we had boys that one year who had the kinds of personality to dance in step with four others. But one can't expect ordinary musicians to become Beethoven and I can't see what good could come out of me trying to teach these boys basketball. I would be disappointed in them and they would feel it and come to resent me. Life is something like that, I think."

"What do you mean?" Jane asked as they had come to their bus stop.

"Now whenever I look back at growing up in the desert I can see patterns, some large and some small. We had no history before nineteen-forty-five because we didn't exist. We made our history and then came to believe in it. We were successful quickly in sports so we came to believe it was natural. Our girls in fact were pretty enough that several had careers in films in Hollywood, perhaps it was nothing more than accident that those girls lived in our town at the same time, just as the man who taught us basketball, but we accepted it as proof that our climate or drinking water or something else had placed us under some favorable sun. Some of our boys were even good enough to have careers in professional sports at the highest level and we accepted it as more proof that we were somehow favored by the stars. But later when you are older and have enough experience to compare things and people to, you see how almost impossible the odds were against something like that happening in one small city. I've never seen it happen again anywhere and of course it never happened again in that town. No more movie queens or professional sportsmen. My theory is that it happened in part because there was no history before us to lower our expectations. When you are conditioned by negative thinking then you almost never are successful. It forms a pattern. There are small and large patterns in life that can't be seen until they are played out. Do you know the American writer Willa Cather?"

"No."

"She's a wonderful writer and she wrote her most famous book about a Czech family who settled in the state of Nebraska, *My Antonia*. She once wrote, '*No one ever recognizes a period until it is behind one, until then it is just everyday life.*' I think she understood the patterns in life we never see until later. I can see now something very unusual happened in our town out in that desert, but I couldn't see it then. Probably few other people saw it either. I know that after the war there were elections here in Czechoslovakia and they were very important. The results were part of a pattern that changed the lives of millions of people, but who could see them at the time? And how strange it is for me to think that American soldiers were here walking over these very stones and who of them could imagine they too were playing out some role in that pattern?"

"What is strange about it?"

Wilson smiled through a frown. "A thought came to me recently and there is probably a pattern in it that I can't see, so I'm not sure whether I ought to be pleased or consider it only another irony of life."

"Don't talk in riddles Wilson, explain yourself."

"My father was a soldier over here during the second world war. He told me once he was with Patton's division and I've considered

the possibility that he was once here in Plzen and now I walk over the same ground he once did."
"If he was with Patton's army then it is quite possible he was here in Plzen, but I see nothing ironic about it."
Wilson bit at his lip. "You never knew my father."
"Of course not, but what if I did, would I have liked him?"
"Probably, most people did. I guess he was an easy man to like."
"You could write to him, couldn't you, and simply ask him if he was in Plzen."
"I might do it, if I knew where he was and if he was alive, but I don't know where he is or if he is alive."
"Why not?"
"Because I don't care. He and my mother split up when I was a teenager and I haven't tried to find him. I got a letter from him once when I was in the army. It was from some town in California, but I never answered it."
"Are you the type who holds grudges, Wilson?"
Wilson glanced at her and smiled. "Never hold a grudge longer than fifty years."
"You're primitive, you know."
Wilson shook his head slowly and bit his lip as their bus pulled into sight. "No, Tozantova, I doubt that I am. I sort of wish I was because it would simplify everything. You'd never have to consider such things as patterns in life or what they mean. You would only have to live for the moment. And if I was really a primitive man I would never ever consider coaching that basketball team, only a sentimental man would."
"So you'll do it?"
"I didn't say that I would. But I like that boy Robert. I think he has something inside him that the boys on my high school team had inside them. A kind of fire to be a champion. I like that. But the others are a sure formula for instant heartburn."
"Well, you know there are both good and bad kinds of primitives, Wilson." Jane Tozantova remarked as they stepped onto their bus.

"Really? I thought you were either a primitive or you were not."

"Don't be simple minded, van Gogh was a primitive man, for example, but he was a good one."

"What about Patton, what kind was he?"

"I'm not sure, but probably a bad primitive."

"Oh, I don't think so. He read poetry you know, even wrote two books of poetry. He was quite a complicated man."

"His profession was killing people."

"Not true. His profession was one of defending people from being killed, a noble profession."

"Well, he was certainly a man who enjoyed his work and that seems to me primitive....Just like you."

"Then you think I'm the bad kind of primitive?"

"I didn't say that."

"But you implied it."

"I'm not sure whether you're a bad or good primitive."

Wilson smiled. "I hope I'm the same kind as Patton. I liked his attitude about life."

"Which was?"

"Never drink with your enemies. Never smoke cheap cigars. Never drink bad whiskey. And kill the son of a bitches before they do it to you."

"You made that up?"

"Maybe."

"You know he had a long love affair with a much younger woman and he was related to her and she committed suicide several weeks after he died?"

"I think I read that once," Wilson admitted. "Like I said, he was a complicated man."

"He was a brute," Jane Tozantova insisted as they sat down. "A primitive brute."

"A complicated man," Wilson repeated softly.

Chapter 8

"My name is Roman Havlicek, I teach biology here and I'd like to invite you to our evening English conversation class. I think you would enjoy some of the students and they want to meet you."

Wilson stood up from his desk and shook the man's hand. As he did he studied his face. Havlicek was a man about his own age, he guessed. He was slightly shorter and of a slighter build. What he found most interesting about him was the sincerity in his voice and eyes.

"I'd be pleased to come."

"Where are you from in America?"

"The state of Washington, do you know where it is?"

"Yes, it's north of Oregon and south of Canada."

Wilson nodded and gestured with a hand for him to sit down at the chair next to his desk.

"Were you a teacher in America?"

"Sort of."

"What do you mean?"

Wilson smiled. "You've never been to America, have you?"

"No, but we've watched German television for years and most of us have listened to the Voice of America and Radio Free Europe for years, so America isn't a mystery to us."

"Things have changed in America, some things have changed very much, such as our schools."

"How have they changed?"

"It's very complicated to explain, maybe we could talk about it another time."

"Are you married?"

"No. I'm divorced. And you?"

Havlicek smiled. "I'm single, but single and committed to someone. Do your parents live in Washington too?"

"My mother died a few years ago and I'm not sure about my father. He and my mother divorced when I was a teenager and I've lost touch with him."

"Have you any brothers or sisters?"

"I had one brother, Phillip, but he died about ten years ago."

"So you are alone?"

Wilson nodded with a smile. "And you?"

"I have a mother in Prague."

Wilson felt a need to change subjects. "So you studied biology at the university and decided to become a teacher?"

"Not exactly. My first love was physics, but they had no need for physics teachers here, they needed a biology teacher and I had also studied biology. I needed a job and I've been here ever since I finished school. It's not a perfect marriage, but in Czechoslovakia there are few perfect marriages in anything and you learn to accept the practical. May I call you David?"

"Of course. Nobody at home calls me Mr. Wilson, not even my students."

"Are you a practical man?" Havlicek asked with a smile that Wilson felt was mischievous.

"Jane Tozantova says I'm primitive," Wilson answered with a smile to match Havlicek's.

"You don't strike me as a practical man, perhaps Jane is right."

"Maybe, but I'd probably be better off if I was more practical."

"There's a need for practical men, but there always a need too for men who are not practical."

"How do you mean?"

"Practical men live out of necessity, they know the limitations of the world, but the world needs men who question the limits, like Einstein. Without men who question and live beyond what is considered practical there's no progress. I would like to be among the kind of men who question and live beyond the practical, but I don't. I teach biology. Biology isn't my first love, not even my second love anymore. I simply do it to make a living. What's your first love in life?"

Wilson wasn't ready for the question, it seemed too personal a thing to be talking about with someone who was a stranger. Havlicek sat smiling, as if continuing a game. "I'm not sure I have one, to tell the truth."

"What subject did you teach in America?"

"I was a high school history teacher."

"Is there a period of history that you like more than others?"

"I'm fond of the Greek history about Athens."

Roman Havlicek smiled politely. "Well, Czechoslovakia doesn't have a reputation as a land of Greek heroes, may I ask why you chose to come here?"

Wilson's instinct was to avoid the question as it seemed once again something too personal to be discussed with a stranger, but an impulse struck him. "I guess I've been in a kind of rut and need a change of scene."

"What's a rut?"

Wilson bit at his lower lip and cocked his head. "I guess I'm not a practical man. Maybe I never have been. So many things changed in America after I finished my studies at the university that I've haven't been able to change with them. A rut is when you are caught up in the same thing and can't change directions. So when the chance came to come here I didn't resist the idea, I needed some change."

"So you didn't come here out of idealism."

Wilson smiled. "I'm afraid not."

"Do you know much about the history of Czechoslovakia?"

"No."

"How long will you stay here?"

"I don't know, I'm not sure it matters one way or the other."

"What do you mean?"

"I haven't a wife or family at home, I have no job I care about waiting for me. There is nothing waiting for me and nothing to get in a hurry about."

"Maybe you'll like it here and stay longer than you think."

Wilson bit at his lip and nodded, as if to concede a point. "Maybe."

A silence fell between them that signalled the end of their conversation. "I'm glad we have an American in our school, maybe you can breathe some fresh air into it."

Wilson felt awkward hearing the sincerity in his voice. "I'm glad to be here too, but I'm not sure I'm the kind of American the school needs."

Havlicek got up and put his hand on the door to leave, then turned and Wilson saw the mischievous smile again, "I'm quite sure you're just the kind of American we need." Then he was gone as quickly as he had turned up.

Chapter 9

He told himself he was ready to accept the idea of losing his first game as basketball coach of Lokomotiva Boys. But, of course, he wasn't ready. The score was only 70-65 and the game was played on the road in Prague, but long after the game was over, as he rode the train back to Plzen, he still felt the tightness in his stomach from replaying the game over in his head. He saw again the sloppy, even thoughtless, passes being thrown away, the timid defense and, most infuriating, the total inability to play together as a team. Almost always when the opposing defense stiffened Lokomotiva broke down in desperation shots or his players broke down into what was called at home "playground" basketball. It was opposite of everything he had learned from his high school coach.

Wilson tried to console himself with the fact they had only three practices and knew only two plays, but the memory of the game still tied his stomach in a knot.

Mental discipline, he knew, was at the heart and soul of every successful team, no matter what the sport. That was the reason for the existence of sports: to learn how to push yourself to a point as close to maximum performance as possible through mental concentration. Thus to breakdown mentally was the worst thing that could happen to a player or team. Losing and winning was merely a by-product of that effort. Winning was always nice, but extending yourself mentally was at the heart of competition. Without that, Wilson thought, sports was as empty of meaning as something such as body building, where people pumped up muscles to create an effect, but where nothing was developed on the interior. It was perhaps natural, Wilson reflected, that body building had become popular in America, not just with men but with women too, and magazines flooded the stands which showed people flexing giant grease smeared muscles. It reflected the triumph of superficiality in the American mind, Wilson thought, and it would surely spread eastward to old Europe as well.

Wilson continued to try to console himself on his train ride by telling himself that if a man had slow feet no coach could give him quick feet, if a man was short no one could make him tall, and if a man had the soul of a mouse you couldn't give him the heart of a lion. But a counter voice argued that a good coach ought to build up a sense of mental discipline either by guile or bluster in his players.

But how, he argued, could you do that when you couldn't speak the language of your players? Reality came down hard on Wilson that he was facing a nearly impossible situation, rather like that he faced years before during his first year of teaching when he had been asked to take over for the sick basketball coach. He had not forgotten those nights when after losing yet another game he felt like throwing up.

It wasn't the losing that brought about the sting, it was having to watch human beings give into something out of resignation, out of lack of spirit, and out of a failure to extend themselves mentally. Being around people like that made him feel uncomfortable. He tried to disguise it when around his players, as he told himself that since they had never been exposed to success they couldn't be blamed for not knowing how to achieve it. He finished the two hour train ride from Prague in silence and tried to force smiles when he shook hands with his players at the train station and said good night. But his smile was the smile of a man who had bit into a lemon.

The next day Wilson boarded an early morning train back to Prague with his team for another game against a really good team, VS Praha. It was a massacre, 99-69. The difference in size and talent was so great the results were predictable, but Wilson agonized as he watched his team break down mentally too many times and made the margin of defeat much larger than he thought it should have been.

On the train ride home he tried once again to console himself with the idea the outcome was beyond his control. But the idea of resigning himself to losing felt repugnant. You lose, he argued, but you never lose your pride and discipline and the spirit to compete on every play. If you lose those things then you'll end up a loser in life too.

Passing a Bohemian village in the night, Wilson broke into a depreciating smile at his reflection in the window of his train compartment. Where had his pride and spirit and mental discipline gotten him in life that he had acquired from sports? It had gotten him aches and pains in his shoulders and knees and a job teaching English in a grimy smoke-stack town thousands of miles from his home.

It was interesting, he reflected, how you learned with time how many of the things people told you were good about life when you were a boy turned out to have little or no value at all in the adult world.

Wilson's smile turned thoughtful as his mind turned to his old friend Father Sedlacek and the Shroud of Turin. Ft. Sedlacek had never said he believed the shroud was authentic but he wasn't shy about handing out literature that said it was. What was the magnet that pulled a man toward a life as a priest? There must have been a powerful force in a man to allow him to believe in something in the world that could in the end be exposed as empty or false. He couldn't find fault with Ft. Sedlacek or anyone else who felt drawn to religion or service in a religious life. In fact, he admired people who could devote so much faith to something on so little hard evidence, often on evidence that later proved to be false, such as the Shroud of Turin proved to be.

That kind of faith never worked for him. At one time he had

A HOME IN BOHEMIA 55

tried it but it never worked out. At Ft. Sedlacek's urging Wilson studied the Bible, but it had the opposite results: he ended up with more questions that he had begun with and more doubts. And he was always given the same remedy by Ft. Sedlacek for his doubts: faith was believing in what couldn't be proven.

Wilson had always felt like a kind of outcast when he accepted invitations from Ft. Sedlacek to attend Catholic Youth retreats in the mountains. It seemed he was always the one who asked the questions at the Bible study sessions which drew long silent stares from the others, then the nervous laughter from the counsellor. And most often the only reason he went in the first place was because he knew a Catholic girl who was going on the retreat who he had some interest in. Wilson's interests were purely secular: girls.

Still, Wilson later agreed to take Catholic instructions during the summer after his freshman year of college, again at the invitation of Ft. Sedlacek. By then Wilson had more doubts about religion than he had as a high school student. During his freshman year of college he had several sexual encounters and one was a liaison with an older woman of twenty-seven. She made no pretence at all of being impressed by Wilson robust athletic appearance nor did she express any desire to develop some kind of deeper relationship. Her interests began and ended in Wilson's services in bed. Being naive Wilson felt compelled to act out rituals he'd learned were necessary to overcome teenage girls.

To his consternation this only seemed to annoy her. Of greater perplexity was the casual way she seemed to use him to satisfy herself. After each encounter he felt a resentment mixed in with growing self-doubts. Clearly there was no interest on her part to fake any interest in his life as a student or what he hoped to do after school or even some exchange of opinions about everyday life. Her attitude became clear to him: I have my life and you have yours and let's not try to mix them up. Still, Wilson couldn't on occasion resist the need to try to draw her into personal conversations and her response became a kind of ritual: she would light a fresh cigarette and ask in a dry voice, "Freshen up my drink, won't you sweetheart?"

It was Wilson who broke off the liaison never sure himself whether it was because of his resentment or self-doubts. During the summer break he asked Ft. Sedlacek how twelve healthy men, such as the apostles, could abstain from sex for a life-time? The priest answered patiently that with baptism the apostles received the grace and protection of the Holy Spirit which removed mortal desires such as sex. Wilson nursed the hope that after taking instructions and receiving baptism that he too would be relieved of such earthly desires - until he was married, at which time he hoped they would mysteriously be restored.

It never worked that way, of course. When he returned to school after the summer break, tan and healthy and full of energy to spill on the football field, he often found himself after football practice thinking about the 27-year old secretary named Rose. And soon he found himself making a visit to her apartment only to discover that she had moved during the summer. But there was no doubt in him mind why he had gone there. It was not to have a discussion or to test his baptism. Later he dwelled on whether he should confess his thoughts to a priest. He didn't.

He confronted the reality that he was much the same David Wilson after baptism that he was before baptism. The thought pricked at him that he was doomed to go through life as a kind of exile from the church and no amount of Bible study or instructions could change his fate. Maybe he was what one of his history professors had called someone, an incorrigible?

His memories brought a frown to his reflection in the window of the train compartment. It seemed obvious that when he studied patterns of his life there was a consistency which lead to certain truths. It wasn't true, for example, to say he was a doubter as an adult. His skeptical character could be seen in his youth. He had often questioned his teachers in high school, sometimes openly, more often silently. He was almost always the one in class who wanted to know why. And after his experience in the Army and Vietnam, his skeptical nature merely grew rather than began. In fact, his attitudes about life had undergone a kind of petrifaction after the Army.

Wilson reasoned that he had ended up on a train to a place called Plzen because he had, as Jane Tozantova suspected, never been practical. Roman Havlicek, the biology teacher at his school, remarked that in Czechoslovakia, you learned to be practical. Yet his first act was to agree to coach a basketball team that was an instant formula for frustration because it had no reasonable chance too be successful. His excuse for this was because he liked a sixteen-year old boy named Robert. That was an act of sentiment out of proportion to reality and it was sentiment in life that always lead a man to trouble.

Wilson studied his reflection in the window of the train more closely. He had never been practical and yet he couldn't claim to be someone exotic or romantic enough to be called primitive, as Jane Tozantova called him. For a real primitive engaging in a liaison with a woman such as Rose would not have suffered any bumps and bruises in his self-image. He had known real primitives on the university football team who bragged about their sexual conquests as casually as some men bragged of their hunting skills for birds or deer. It was the same when he was in the Army, he'd met numerous soldiers who claimed to have performed prodigious sexual acts with women without any sentiment or emotional involvement. Yet Wilson couldn't engage in such liaisons without some sentiment or being caught in some emotional web. And if you couldn't be practical in life and you hadn't thick enough skin to be primitive, there were few options. It seemed you had to be one or the other. If not you lived in a no man's land where the only end was failure, or worse, a comic ending. A Quixote ending.

Reviewing his past a swell of self-doubt invaded Wilson. The boys of Lokomotiva basketball team were the practical ones: they didn't agonize about losing because they accepted the fact the other teams were better. It was the Czech nature, Wilson was told often by Czechs, to be practical and accept reality. It was why they didn't take up arms against the Nazis in 1938 when Hitler stole the Sudetland, it explained why they voted in such numbers for the communists in 1946 and why later they didn't resist the Russian invasion in 1968 with more than passive resistance. Czechs had learned to be practical people, to make velvet revolutions, and maybe he had more to learn from them than he could ever teach their children. If anyone asked him about what he'd learned from sports he could only answer that he'd gotten painful joints.

Sports hadn't taught him how to be a successful husband, it had not even taught him how to be a successful lover to a woman like Rose, when all she had wanted was a man to provide the most basic of services. If only, Wilson thought, he was truly primitive he could follow his basic instincts and become something as commonplace as a successful football coach in a small town and marry and become content with life in a middle-class way. Or he could have gone another direction, as had many of the football boys had who he had played with at the university, and become businessmen determined to become wealthy without regard to the fine points of rules or regulations, like the Reagan Republicans who believed in the every man for himself code.

And if he had the soul of a practical man he could have followed the road to success of so many of his colleagues in education who worked their way up the administrative ladder to become bureaucrats on nothing more than the force of hot air, which found its way into the idiotic directives that filtered down to those sterile vapid Monday afternoon staff meetings.

You had to be one or the other in life. If not you ended up riding trains in the middle of the night in places like Bohemia.

Wilson broke his pencil into and tossed the ends at the waste basket hung on the wall next to him. Several of the boys who had been half-dozing blinked awake at the sound and stared at him in consternation. He stood and pushed open the sliding door of his compartment and entered the passageway and stood staring out the window.

Chapter 10

Fridays became Wilson's day of liberation. On Friday afternoons he went to a gym in the Doubravka section in Plzen and played basketball with a group of men who at one time had played basketball for the Lokomotiva Club. Their age and bulging waist lines had graduated them into the senior's division. They scrimmaged in friendly matches against a group of younger men who were on the Lokomotiva Club basketball team.

It was an escape for Wilson from his solitary runs along the streets of Plzen, but the Friday matches were not without an element of frustration. His pent up hunger for competition, even in a meaningless practice game against men, who in most cases were twenty years younger than him and his teammates, flushed his frustration to the surface. Though far from being in the physical condition he would like to be in, Wilson was still the best conditioned and skilled athlete on the old boy's team. He steamed relentlessly up and down the basketball court as if determined to punish himself, but there wasn't punishment in it instead a sense of exhilaration. He felt a kind of elixir in stretching muscles he hadn't used in years and the feel of being soaked in his own sweat along with the discomfort of getting enough energy for another charge down the court awoke memories of happy times in his athletic past. He basked in the feel of jostling, shoving, elbowing and bumping for position under the basket for a rebound.

The winner was the first side to reach 100. Wilson, of course, always knew what the score was and had a keener interest in winning than most of the other players. When one of his teammates was careless with a pass which resulted in an easy basket for the quicker and younger opponents, he sometimes forgot himself and swore loudly enough for everyone to hear. The idea of losing, even to men twenty years younger, was unthinkable to him.

His occasional outbursts of frustration with his ponderous teammates were but minor irritants in comparison to the pleasure he had of being able to throw himself without reserve into physical competition. Afterward the older veterans and the younger men showered and joined together in a group at the neighborhood *hostinec,* which was always smoke filled and crowded with a Friday after work throng. There the basketballers had a section of the tavern reserved and a half dozen tables were shoved together to form a train along one wall where they drank mugs of Plzner beer, argued in loud voices, played cards, sang songs and enjoyed the comraderie that sport competition and beer bring out in men. Though Wilson could understand little of the language he soaked up, he savored the feel of fellowship.

It was like a song, he thought once as he drank from his mug of beer and ran his eyes over the faces in the beer hall. The rise and fall of the old language in his ears, the faces, the voices, the cadence of the songs, even the smoky air, had a feel of something foreign and old. Taken together it was a Bohemian song, he thought, though he wasn't sure how to define what was Bohemian. It was old and different and after his exhausting wars on the court with the younger players, sometimes with his own players, and always the relentless war with himself to push toward some unknown point, he felt soothed to sit quietly and absorb the Bohemian song of beer and men and smoke and noise.

Sometimes a man with an accordion was at the beer hall and listening to him play and seeing the unrestrained pleasure in his face Wilson felt something unknown, something close to contentment.

Chapter 11

"So how is your basketball team doing?" Roman Havlicek asked as he peeled an undersized looking orange.

Wilson looked across his desk at Havlicek who sat slouched, legs crossed and a contented house cat expression on his face. "How do you know I coach a basketball team?"

Havlicek smiled. "Everybody knows everybody's business in this school. Who is sleeping with who, how much money you make, if your plumbing is working or not. I hear your toilet leaks, your kitchen faucet leaks, you haven't found anyone to sleep with yet and that three of your students have fallen in love with you."

"My toilet and sink still leak, none of my students have fallen in love with me, and I'm not looking for anyone to sleep with."

"I don't believe it. I think a man with red blood like yours is always looking for a woman to sleep with."

Wilson laughed. "Red blood like mine? I guess my blood is about the same as anyone elses."

"No, I don't think so. That would be like saying everyone has the same kind of soul."

"Who has seen a soul, have you?"

"No, of course not. There are many things I haven't seen. Radiation for example. Do you know much about radiation?"

"A little," Wilson answered.

"Well, you can't see it, but it's real enough to kill people. We can only measure it's existence with instruments. So how do we measure a human soul?"

Wilson leaned back in his chair and studied Havlicek without making a reply, as if to say to him, the stage is yours. Havlicek popped a slice of orange in his mouth and took the cue. "To determine the nature of souls is to answer the question of human existence - the question that is above all other questions. Do you know much about Einstein?"

"Some."

"The last twenty years of his life he spent trying to solve the riddle of quantum mechanics in which particles seem to be incompatible with laws of gravity, but he wasn't able to succeed. Some scientists believe particles as big as brain cells can jump from one energy state to another and that has something to do with the act of creative thinking. So what is so strange about the concept of a soul?"

"You've lost me."

"If particles can traverse space without our understanding of how or why then the idea of something like an energy state such as a soul can't be rejected. And it follows as logical that if the energy of a soul is real then there must be different levels of energy in different souls, just as there is in all masses. Haven't you ever given any serious thought to the question of souls?"

"I'm not a scientist, so I don't know anything about quantum mechanics or laws of physics. And I'm not a philosopher, so I don't spend any time wondering about souls."

Havlicek grinned, as if enjoying the mental sparring. "Of course you do. You've admitted Greek history is your favorite period and it's foundation is based upon the fact the Greeks loved above all order and logic. I'd guess you're also Greek in your thinking and to imagine you have no opinion on human souls is a contradiction."

Wilson bit his lip and sighed. "Okay, I've thought about the idea of a soul, but the more I thought about it, the more doubts I had. And finally I decided the whole idea is nothing more than man's attempt to soften the reality that there is nothing after this life."

"You said your brother died, how did he die."

"Some people think he died from radiation exposure."

"How?"

"We grew up next to the world's first atomic bomb factory. In the beginning no one knew what it was because of military secrecy. But after the war they told people there was no danger from it and people believed them. But they didn't tell the truth. There were radiation leaks from the very beginning, but we didn't find out about them until nineteen-eighty-six when certain government documents became declassified. We learned many of the leaks weren't accidental, but were military experiments. So I guess we were the guinea pigs and some didn't survive. I guess Phil was one of them. He got cancer of the thyroid and before it was diagnosed it spread and they couldn't save him."

"How long ago was it?"

"About ten years ago."

"I'm sorry."

"Oh, I don't think about it much anymore."

"What was your brother like, do you mind talking about him?"

"No I don't mind. Phil was my younger brother. He was always cheerful, kind of happy go lucky and a good husband. It always seemed to me he was the one who had everything to live for, he had a good wife, two kids, and he liked his work."

Wilson opened a drawer of his desk and removed a manila folder and handed Havlicek several newspaper clippings from the folder. "Take a look at these, they tell a story that you don't find in the history books and which ordinary people don't believe."

Havlicek took the clippings and began reading. They were from an American newspaper and told about radiation leaks at Hanford. One story was headlined,

"SOME BABIES NEAR HANFORD GOT
TWICE CHERNOBYL DOSE."

Havlicek sighed and handed the clippings back to Wilson. "I had no idea things like that happened in America. Here, yes, Russia

66 A HOME IN BOHEMIA

yes, but not in America."

"Not many people outside of Oregon and Washington know about Hanford or even care. They don't care because they don't think it touches their lives. Hanford is three thousand miles from New York and the suffering it caused is out of sight. The people who died and will die from it are nothing more than statistics to people who live in places like New York or Los Angeles. Probably not more than one American in a thousand knows about Hanford. They'll know about it when the bill comes to clean it up because half of all the nuclear waste in America is buried there and it'll take about fifty years. It has made me think a lot about what the difference is between our government and the Russians, who we were always told were the bad guys. Maybe under the business suits we're not as different as we tell people we are."

Wilson took another newspaper clipping from his desk drawer and handed it to Havlicek.

"East Germany's former Stalinist regime secretly guillotined 62 political prisoners and burned their bodies in the 1950s, according to the state crematorium in Dresden."

"I found that in an American newspaper last May. I knew, of course, those kind of crimes happened everywhere the communists took over, so it was no great revelation to me. But this story wouldn't go away. I read it at the same time a man asked me to come here. Then I read another story about Hanford."

Wilson handed Havlicek another clipping. "It's about a man named Ernest Johnson. He died in 1948 from a radiation burn at Hanford but the government wanted it kept secret so they falsified his autopsy to read he died from a heart attack. His wife found out the truth and tried to get them to correct it. The government boys got pretty nasty. One man quoted in the story put it this way, 'We were told to keep our mouths shut and not ask questions. So we didn't.' I guess I'm the kind of guy who never knew when to keep his mouth shut and I always asked questions. I figured those people who got guillotined in Dresden were probably the same as me and that's when I made up my mind to come to Plzen, after I read that article."

"Good men are supposed to ask questions."

"Says who?"

"Your friend Plato, for one.'

"And smart men are supposed to know when to keep their mouths shut," Wilson added.

"Sure some men who ask questions end up like Socrates, if that's what you mean. Have you ever heard of a Czech man named Jan Patocka?"

"No."

"An interesting man, but few people in the West know about him. He was a philosophy professor. When the Germans were here they wouldn't let him teach, after the war he got his job back at Charles University in Prague only to be suspended by the communists in nineteen-forty-eight. Then in sixty-eight, during the Dubcek years, he got his job back only to be suspended once again when the Russians invaded. I was living in Prague then and went to some of his lectures, I snuck in, I suppose, since I'd finished my studies. Patocka was already a kind of legend, though few in my age group understood fully what he represented. We just knew that the Germans banned him and the communists too, so we felt he must be important to hear. He also liked Greek history and had written a book on Aristotle which managed to get published, though most everything else was censored. He wrote that freedom doesn't come after the struggle is over, but during the battle, when those involved become freer than those who refuse to get involved. The solidarity of the shattered, is what he called it. These people form a solidarity at the front, he wrote, and only they grasp the real meaning of life and death."

"What happened to him after the revolution?"

"Patocka died long before the revolution came." Havlicek's face lost its serious expression and a trace of a smile returned. "Even though you say it no longer hurts to talk about your brother, when you talk about him I feel some anger in your voice. Am I wrong?"

"I'd just like some truth. I'd like to see those who were responsible for poisoning people be held accountable in public. We're supposed to teach students in our schools they're responsible for their behavior and then we read everyday in newspapers where people in our government make immoral decisions and we can't even find out who they are. It makes teaching seem empty and useless."

"You still think about him a lot, don't you?"

"There are some things you can't let go of until some justice has been served."

"I know the feeling."

"What do you mean?"

"I lost a relative too."

"Who?"

Havlicek became thoughtful and Wilson for first time he saw an expression of caution in his face. "I lost my father."

"How?"

"He was an American soldier!"

"Are you sure of it?"

"My mother was sure of it."

"What I meant was...."

"I think I know what you meant,"

"What happened to him?"

"My mother was very young then, nine-teen. She met him during the summer of forty-five, but by November of that year all the Americans had been transferred out of Bohemia."

"What do you know about your father?"

"He was an enlisted man, about twenty-five."

"Why didn't they get married?"

"They sent him back to America and discharged him because

he...."

"Did he know she was pregnant?"

"No, I don't think so."

"You don't sound bitter."

"I'm not."

"What kind of a son of a bitch would leave a nineteen-year-old girl if he really loved her?"

"Well, he didn't abandon her or run off, he was sent away. And like thousands of other soldiers he was lonely. It was a time of turmoil here and everywhere in Europe. American and Russian and Czech politics got all mixed together and one pregnant woman and one soldier were not important to anyone."

"I'm not sure I'd have the same attitude as you."

"You learn to be practical" Havlicek answered with a smile.

"Do you ever wonder anymore about him, like if he is alive?"

"Of course, I even wonder if I might have a brother or sister in America."

"Sometimes I think you're better off not knowing much about people."

"What do you mean?"

"When we're young I think we all imagine our fathers are heroes, but then we grow up and discover what kind of people they really are."

"What kind of man was your father?"

"A loser."

"A loser?"

"That's what we call someone without any character."

"You sound like someone who is bitter."

"No, not at all, I haven't cared about him for a long time."

"But you must have cared once."

"Sure. My father was a man everyone seemed to like. He was a hunter, fisherman, gambler, drinker, a hard worker, but one day he didn't come home. So my mother raised me and Phil alone."

"You mean he simply abandoned your family?"

"Exactly. No note or letter or discussion, just disappeared. I always thought he probably hit it big in some card game and took off for a place like Reno."
"What's Reno?"
"A town in the state of Nevada that's famous for gambling."
"Your father was a gambler?"
"Nope, but he thought he was. He was just a construction worker and a kind of small town gambler who knew cards well enough to win some money from small town men who didn't know cards. So I always figured he won a big pot one night and was drunk enough to take off for some bigger town and kept on drinking and gambling and ended up on the skids somewhere."
"Didn't you ever try to find him?"
"No."
"It sounds cold-blooded."
"Maybe, but when I was young it hit me hard, then when I got old enough to look for him I was at the point I just didn't care anymore and I never looked back."
"So with your mother and father and brother gone, you're alone."
"I guess that's the way it worked out."
"Who can understand the way life works? I was standing at my office window the morning you walked up the front steps of our school. I saw you and somehow I knew you were the American people said was coming. I was happy because I thought, now things will be more interesting here. I think Jane Tozantova was right, you know."
"Right about what?"
"That you have a primitive nature."
"That's crap."
"No, I believe it."
"Don't believe it, it's crap."
"You must have read some of Plato's ideas, so you probably know this quote from him, *'There are men who have an intuitive insight, which causes them to do good and beautiful things. They*

themselves do not know why they do as they do and therefore they are unable to explain to others. It is so with poets and with all good men.'"

Havlicek stood and strolled to the door with the air of a lawyer who had delivered a closing argument to a jury and was confident he had made a winning delivery. "I think Plato was speaking about the nature of souls. Some men are primitive because they are born with that way. And nothing can be done to change it. I think the best men are primitive."

Havlicek closed the door behind him.

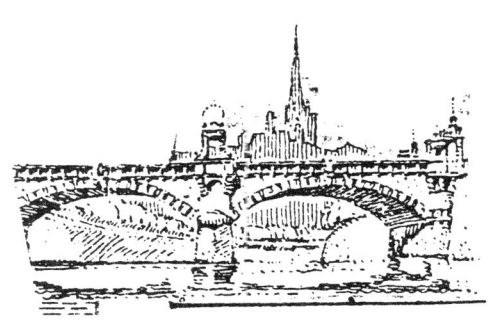

Chapter 12

Wilson sat watching television on a Saturday morning as President Bush spoke to the Czechoslovakian Parliament in Prague. Everyone seemed pleased and often erupted into applause when Mr. Bush mentioned human rights and how the American government would not abandon the Czechoslovakian people this time.

It was difficult to believe this was the same president who Wilson had watched on television in America only a few months before. Then the small Baltic country Lithuania had asked President Bush to recognize them as a free and independent nation and he had retreated into silence and when he broke his silence weeks later he said, through a spokesman, that he had nothing to say about Lithuania "because he didn't want to make the wrong mistake." That day there was no mention of human rights and the president of Lithuania compared Mr. Bush to Neville Chamberlain.

It was all theater, Wilson knew. The audience wanted to hear a certain kind of script read with the ending already known, and like a Shakespeare play, it sent everyone home satisfied. It was a kind of fairy tale in which everyone agreed to suspend reality while photographers flashed cameras and television crews sent selected clips back home via satellite, showing a smiling president and happy Czechs. A *"pohodka"* for the global village. Good theater.

Wilson shifted his attention to Czechoslovakian President Vaclav Havel, who sat slightly to the right and above Mr. Bush. When the television camera panned Havel his expression didn't reveal whether he was impressed or merely amused with the theater.

A HOME IN BOHEMIA 73

Havel was wearing an earphone to receive the translation from English, but Wilson thought Havel's expression would have been exactly the same without the headset: Havel had seen enough theater and written enough plays that the script being read at the moment was no more or no less important than any other script.

Havel chose the right mask for the moment, a trace of a smile, his eyes centered on the speaker, polite applause at the right moment, a fuller smile when President Bush quoted from Havel's writing and turned to recognize him. But Wilson understood Havel knew Bush's history as an old apparatchik and as someone once wrote, apparatchiks in communists countries would be apparatchiks in western countries and the apparatchiks in western countries would be the same if they were living in communists countries.

Maybe it is a matter of blood, Wilson thought. Men the world over are much the same; the names might be different as well as the languages, but they do what they do, as Plato said, by instinct. Havel and Bush were two different kinds of men because they had different kinds of blood. Havel knew it. But Bush probably didn't know it. Living for so long in an artificially controlled environment of politically appointed jobs and reading scripts penned by flacks of the same instincts as Hollywood writers, Bush became like a flower nurtured in a hot house where the temperature was carefully controlled. Havel on the other hand had survived the chill winds of real life.

Somewhere in the blood of each man, Wilson speculated, must be something genetic that pulled each in a different direction. Havel had reason to wear an ever so slight smile of amusement as he listened to an old politician reading from Havel's writing and pretending to believe it. Good theater.

Wilson recalled some of Havel's words he had read: "Dissident do not choose to be dissidents the way one decides to be a tailor or a blacksmith. Instead the inner logic of their thinking, behavior or work leads them to dissidence...."

Havel exposed a hard truth: no one really chooses to be anything in life, they are born to it.

Wilson stood and turned off the television before the end of Bush's speech and looked out his sixth floor window toward a ridge just beyond the eastern edge of Plzen. His mind turned to his basketball team. They had a game late in the afternoon. There wasn't much doubt what the results would be. Lokomotiva had already played the team once, before Wilson had become coach and Lokomotiva had lost by about twenty points. The team they had lost to was not a particularly good team. They were an average team, but they did play as a team, so they had easily defeated Lokomotiva. And they would win again. Probably the score would be closer, but it would be just as ugly. There would be the usual errant passes, the standing and watching when they should be moving their feet, and when they did run too often they would run to the wrong spot on the court. Lokomotiva would make just enough mistakes to make it a routine win for the visiting team.

The two teams were roughly equal in talent, but the difference was in organization. Mental organization. Wilson had reduced his plays down to their most basic elements to eliminate as many mental errors as possible. But he discovered what he most feared, even when they could understand the system the mental discipline to perform with consistency was lacking in his group of players. So there was little any coach could do with them, even a coach who spoke Czech.

Standing at his window with a view over looking the Bohemian landscape Wilson felt a mixture of emotions. He liked most of the boys. None of them were problem boys. You couldn't dislike a boy for having slow feet or a slow mind. But to have to witness them day after day failing to push themselves mentally to become better drove a stake into his heart. He remembered playing basketball for his high school and the moments when there was only silence in the locker room after a practice because everyone had worked so hard they were but a single step from exhaustion and he remembered the same dry gut feel in the locker room after

A HOME IN BOHEMIA 75

football practice in college. He never forgot one player in particular on the football team who had to be carried off the practice field with an injury and how he had cried openly in front of the other players, not from the pain of his injury but from knowing he would no longer be a part of the team. The closeness athletes form when they endure trials and then triumphs together cements a bond that remains in memory without end. The idea of being a part of a team that was only going through the motions left him in turmoil. He knew from the beginning it was a mistake to agree to coach them, he tried to tell Jane Tozantova. "What good can come of it? I would be disappointed in them and they would feel it and come to resent me."

Wilson felt it was coming true. He felt his attitude hardening toward them. And he sensed they felt it. He had always been that way, he admitted. He had never formed friendships with people he sensed he could not count on to push themselves. He could act politely toward them but he found ways to distance himself from them that were subtle but effective. It was wrong perhaps, but he found he could not change and least of all he could not pretend.

The basketball team brought Wilson into conflict with a larger question. He had often heard from Czechs themselves the theory there was something odd in Czech character, it centered on their long history of compromising with evil, "of being practical," and accepting rather than actively resisting. Wilson had dismissed the idea. People were good and bad everywhere and he doubted one country had any more or any less of good or bad character in its population.

Standing at his window and looking out over the green landscape and gentle hills, it struck Wilson that he would have to find some Czech history books in English. He was forced to realize how little he knew about the period of Czech history between the time the American Army liberated Plzen and parts of Bohemia in 1945 and the national elections in 1946. What actually happened in those months? How did it happen that the American soldiers were stopped just beyond the hills outside his window and how did it happen that they were removed from Bohemia after only a few months? It seemed strange that after so much suffering during the war that so many Czechoslovakians could vote for a system, such as communism, which had been built on blood and suffering. But, of course, the Czechs unlike Poland did not fight in the war and the percentage of people in France and Italy who voted for the communist party was almost as high.

Wilson made the decision he would have to search for some books to make sense out of the history. There seemed to him an enigma about the people he was surrounded by, such as the boys on his basketball team. And such as Roman Havlicek. There was nothing in Havlicek's face that Wilson could detect as different from a normal Czech face. But if Havlicek told the truth then he wasn't just Czech, but half American. Did that change his character any? Wilson made a second decision to scrutinize Havlicek more carefully.

Nothing seemed to make much sense about the country Wilson found himself living in and the people added to the puzzle. It was lodged between East and West. He could feel in the facades of the old buildings something rooted in the West, but the language had a different feel and rhythm to it than anything he had ever heard. It was something Eastern. And perhaps a nation's language had a larger influence on the character and spirit of a people than was understood.

Wilson continued standing at the window thinking about the people and the land he was living in, then heaved in resignation having arrived at the reality of the basketball game that evening. He felt his whole system stiffen in revolt at the idea of facing another defeat.

Chapter 13

At Roman Havlicek's English class Wilson noticed Martina Bellekova only as one face among the faces of strangers. At the second class he noticed a quality in her voice that triggered what felt to him an old awakening inside him. It was so vague but distinct that he fumbled with the sensation as it circulated in him and he began to steal glances at her. Before the next class meeting Wilson was aware he found himself looking forward to seeing Martina Bellekova.

The awakened emotion confused him. She wasn't at first glance a striking woman, the kind he would fix on in a crowd. Her face was one that blended in easily with others. Her hair was dark and shoulder length. Her mouth was more full than thin. She had a habit of twisting a strand of hair under the curve of her chin as she listened to the instructor. Her voice was a little high and so soft that at times he had to strain at her words. Wilson felt something girlish about her that made him feel she was younger than she was. From Havlicek he found out she was past thirty, though Wilson thought she looked younger.

She was intellectual looking, he thought, without looking dry or stuffy, maybe there was even something sensual looking about her, he speculated. He could not remember being attracted to such a woman, but there was no doubt after he had seen her at the third class meeting he was attracted to her. It puzzled him because it came unexpectedly and there was nothing in his past to prepare him for it. He could understand being attracted to a striking woman, he had even expected it would happen. He had experience with that. He even expected a time would come when he'd meet some Czech woman with a quality that he was attracted to that would ignite something. It might then blossom into a mutual attraction and from there develop into a relationship. He had experience with that. Next, he had learned, almost always, came pain. It could be painful to him or painful to her or painful to both of them at the same time. He had lots of experience with that. It was as if there was something in Wilson that attracted women who felt deeply and also something in his nature that drew him to those kinds women. He had plenty of experience with that. Martina Bellekova also puzzled him because he thought he knew everything about his sexual feelings, she was a reminder that he didn't know everything. He tried to argue that it was only the strain of living in a culture and place that was strange to him and it had somehow altered his chemistry and that had jolted his thinking out of line. But that argument failed to bring him relief.

Maybe it was something more complicated than that. Maybe when a man turned his back upon his native land, when he had passed by too many chances for a practical life, and ventured too far outside of where he belonged, then the world had a license to afflict him with contradictions. And maybe the ultimate enigma the world can afflict on a man is to torture him with an attraction to a woman who is outside his understanding.

Wilson reasoned it must be some kind of challenge he had to face up to. When he felt challenged there was only one way he knew how to react: to harden himself against whatever it was that challenged him. It was the way he had succeeded in sports and the way he had trained to run in the desert under a boiling sun. It was all he knew.

Still he remembered Mary Kennedy. He remembered the sleepless nights and how all his will hadn't helped in that struggle. Hardening yourself against the attraction to a woman was not like being successful in sports.

Accepting the reality that he was connected to a woman unlike any he had felt any attraction to before, he felt a sense of defeat.

Everything about the land he found himself in was strange to him. He allowed himself a smile thinking back to his conversation with Father Sedlacek and his appeal to come to Plzen and reply, "If I wanted to change my life why not just go to Russia."

He had heard that day on television there was food rationing in Moscow and Leningrad. Nothing seemed to work there any longer So things could be worse, couldn't they, you could be in Moscow.

Things aren't hopeless. With enough time you can teach some boys how to play basketball, maybe not this group, but some younger boys. And as strange as the language seems, with enough time you can learn the hang of it. And this thing with Martina Bellekova, in time, it will make some sense or pass away. So get into a long distance frame of mind you need to run in the desert. Try to focus on something in the future, like you do when you're running on a hot day. Then you don't notice the heat - so much.

But this was a different kind of heat, Wilson thought, as he lay on his back in his bed on a Saturday morning and stared at the ceiling. He did not feel confidence in his plan. Affairs with women involved a different chemistry than a football match or running through the desert under a wilting sun. Affairs with women were outside of laws he had read about or understood. No one seemed to have solutions to affairs with women. Not Napoleon or King Solomon or General Patton.

Once a woman found her way into a man's subconscious then all laws and plans were useless. When a man wanted a woman the feeling began in his stomach and worked its way upward, like thinking of Martina Bellekova in bed beside him, her hair falling over her shoulders, the soft feel of her breasts as they flattened against him. Wilson had experience with the feeling. It always started low and ended up near his heart, then it felt like a fist closed around his heart. He had plenty of experience with that - before he came to Plzen.

Wilson bit at his lower lip as he stared at the ceiling. He felt listless and tired as if he had just finished a long run. The discontent he felt was the same nagging discontent he felt the morning when he read in the newspaper about the political prisoners who were guillotined in Dresden. There always seemed something inevitable about a man's fate that he couldn't change or escape.

Chapter 14

Wilson forced himself to roll onto his side and pushed himself into a sitting position with left elbow, to avoid the pain in his right shoulder joint. The right shoulder was always more painful in first morning than the left. But that morning the left shoulder was also sore and it forced him to wince. He stood and was pleased to find there was hardly any pain in his right knee.

His team had a game that Saturday morning against a team from Prague. They were a tall team, people said they were the best team in the league. He remembered too well the first time they had played against them in Prague. They lost by 30 points. While he conceded the Prague team was larger and more disciplined than his team, watching them carefully he thought their big men weren't really good athletes. They were just big.

In his mind he believed smaller, but quicker and more intelligent players could frustrate them with switching aggressive defensive tactics. He had seen it work often in American basketball, even at the professional level. In the end the bigger team would almost always win, but it was possible for Lokomotiva to make it a close contest. And, as he had seen often in America, sometimes a weaker team could "steal" a game from a better team if they could pressure the better team into losing their composure and get them out of their rhythm.

He remembered reading once where an American basketball coach said, "We practice every day at two speeds, one fast and one slow. Because teams are like people. A man shaves every day at a certain speed, but if he is forced to shave faster than he is used to, he cuts himself. Some men like to shave quickly, but if you slow them down then they also can cut themselves. We try to find the speed which the other team doesn't feel comfortable playing at." Wilson had remembered the coach's theory because it seemed so practical and he also remembered the coach's team won the college championship that year.

During the week Wilson tried, through the translation help of Robert, to explain to his team the concept of slowing the game down to frustrate the larger team. The idea was to pass the ball at least five times before shooting. Even with five passes that should leave them with time before the shot clock expired. It wasn't a tactic Wilson felt comfortable with. He liked to meet an opponent or objective head on and try to wear them down with stamina and will. But this situation required practicality: slowing the game down was the only way to avoid another humiliation.

After shaving he slipped into the same shirt and tie he always wore to the games and although neither had brought any good luck to him or the team he stuck with his habit. Then he rode the elevator down and walked out to a frosty morning. His tram was crowded with Saturday morning shoppers, as usual, and he had to reach up to grip the overhead rail, which brought a wince to him. He still missed the pleasure of going to a cafe in the mornings and setting over coffee and a newspaper, he thought as the tram rolled down the grade toward the cluster of buildings that was the city center. He scanned the rows of faces in the coach, as he always did. Sometimes there was one face interesting enough that he would think about it during the day. Faces in Plzen seemed to him to escape any pattern that he could detect. There was a trace of a pattern that he thought he could see in the faces of some of his students that extended out into the general population, but it was easily broken into countless other patterns in a street car full of faces. He thought he felt a strain of something German in Plzen faces that he could not feel when he traveled to Prague.

Connected to one end of the basketball hall was a snack bar. Its customers were mostly young beer drinkers, but it was too early for the beer drinkers and Wilson sat alone at a table with coffee and his basketball play book. It wasn't practical to hope they could steal a game from a team as big as this one from Prague, but maybe they could slow them down enough early that by the time they got into rhythm the game would be almost over and the Lokomotiva boys could learn enough from the tactic that the lesson would carry over to the next game. As his high school coach had told him, even in defeat a team or a man can learn something to make them better.

Wilson's hopes were quickly dashed. The score by the end of the first half was almost identical to the half-time score in their first game at Prague. It was as if Lokomotiva players had not practiced a slow down game at all. They came down and, without a trace of conscience, fired up long shots, short shots and in between shots without bothering to pass two or three times let alone the five passes Wilson had drilled them on in practice. As the score mounted, Wilson's stomach became tighter and tighter until he exploded at a referee. One of the Prague players had rode the back of his player for a rebound and knocked him to the floor, then to add insult to injury his player was whistled for a foul. It was too much. Wilson shot out of his chair and bellowed at the closest official. He did not use any obscene language but the tone of his voice carried throughout the gym and the official, no doubt thinking Wilson had yelled something obscene at him, felt compelled to flash the signal for a technical foul.

Wilson was only irritated at the referee, his despair was with his team. They were going into the tank, he thought, over and over. They were lying down. Following the technical foul, he yelled at one of his players, "Don't let the son of a bitch post up low, that's your territory and you've got to keep the bastard out of there!"

He knew his player had no idea what he had yelled, but his frustration had boiled over at his team's performance. Mercifully the visiting coach began substituting early in the second half and the final score was only a sixteen point difference, instead of the thirty points of the first match. But if ever a score was misleading, Wilson knew, it was the score of that game. The final margin could have just as easily been a forty point difference. Wilson was in despair.

He had simplified everything to the bone. It could get simpler. It was no longer a problem of language, he realized sitting in the snack bar after the game drinking a beer. The problem was one of heart and will. They had never been winners and did not think they ever could be, so they saw no reason to try. It became every man for himself. It meant more to each player to score a basket than it did to do the little things, such as pass to a teammate and screen for him and play tough defense, that won games for a team.

Wilson was pushed up against a truth. The best a coach could hope for with this team was to "graduate" the older players with the worst team attitude. They would graduate by virtue of being too old to play another season at the Junior level. But by then, Wilson reflected with a grim smile, he would also be gone. So it would be only a losing season filled with frustration and indigestion. It wasn't the damn losing, Wilson thought again for the hundredth time, it was the refusal to struggle and push themselves that hurt. Oh sure it was just a game. But so was life. You had to fight back and defend some things in real life - and struggle. Just because someone was taller or bigger and wanted your piece of the floor did not mean that you surrendered it to him without a fight. In life some people bigger might want your property and you had to defend it. You could always shake hands after a basketball game, but until then you went to war with the man who wanted your property just as you would with a thief who broke into your home.

The other truth Wilson was pushed up against was that the team had no leader on the floor to settle them down and to mold them into a unit rather than an undisciplined collection of individuals. Robert was the logical team leader because he was the point guard, but he was too young to lead by experience and he was too small to intimidate with size, as a leader on a team sometimes had to do. To complicate the problem Robert was the only player on the team who had both the skill and intelligence to lead, but he was the team wit. Unable to understand the dialogue between the players, Wilson could still detect by the tone of voice and the laughter who had the sharpest and quickest wit. It was Robert.

Yet Wilson was sure that under the surface of Robert's personality was a serious side, the wit merely hid it and Robert understood his role on the team and fulfilled it. So the team was leaderless on the floor.

"Welcome home, brother," Wilson whispered and tried to smile, but it turned into a grimace. His assistant and the former coach, George, understood the grimace. "I know these boys four years. No good boys. Individual technique o.k. No combination. No good boys."

George finished by waving his big right hand as if a traffic cop flagging cars at a busy intersection. George was nearly a chain smoker and had a habit sliding his pack of cigarettes to Wilson before lighting up and Wilson almost always slid it back without taking one.

Wilson had at first thought he would be glad to see George leave the team because in addition to not knowing much about basketball, he was constantly bellowing remarks at the boys not only in practice but in their games that sounded like insults and the way some of the boys yelled back it made Wilson sure they were insults. But Wilson found himself liking the big man despite his blustery side, and if George was a buffoon, in Jane Tozantova's words, then at least he was a likeable buffoon.

George slid his pack of cigarettes over the table to Wilson and lit his cigarette and held up two fingers to the waiter to signal for two more beers.

Wilson took a cigarette and slid the pack back to George with a half smile. He was the coach of a collection of misfits, he thought, welcome home brother. It didn't make much sense, Wilson thought, looking at the big happy face of George. Drinking his second beer of the day, he saw little hope that it could become better. It could always get worse, he thought, but he couldn't understand how it could get any better. The only thing he knew was that no matter how bad it got you could never quit. Like basketball, sometimes you just had to struggle. It was man's fate.

Chapter 15

"Do you think there will be a war in the Gulf?" Roman Havlicek asked Wilson in his office.

Wilson took another sip of his coffee and thought about it. "No, after the first week I never thought there would be a war."

"How can you be so sure?"

"I'm not," Wilson said looking across his desk at Havlicek.

"Then why do you think there won't be a war when the United Nation's deadline for Iraq to leave Kuwait is less than a month away?"

"Men like Bush have no experience running a war. It's a little like starting a private business - you can go broke in a hurry for reasons you can never predict. We have a strange government, our Congress is a collection of men who have virtually no experience in private business, yet they write the laws about business. Our national government is always broke and they always have to borrow money. No real business could exist like that. So we have a fantasy in America, everyone pretends our government works, but no one really believes it anymore. But in a war there are things that can't be pretended away and you have to have men with experience who know what they're doing."

"Were you ever in a war?"

"I was in Vietnam and I saw war, but I wasn't a soldier out in the field. So I can't claim I know war. I think only the soldier in the field can know war. Only when a man has his belly against the ground because another man is shooting at him and he can smell burnt gun powder in the air and see the face of a friend next to him take a hit, only that man can say he knows war. Flying an airplane at twenty thousand feet and never seeing the face of those you drop bombs on isn't war. War, to my way of thinking, is made only by soldiers who have to get close enough to the enemy to smell him. Then a man knows war. The people at the top of the American government don't know war and they don't know how to run a business. I think they will make a deal in the Gulf to avoid a war."

"You sound sure of it."

"No, I'm not sure of it. I wouldn't bet a dime on it. I heard last night on German television that nine-hundred thousand Americans lost jobs in the past five months. And it is expected to get worse. More banks have gone out of business in America in the last two years than in anytime since the depression of the nine-teen thirties. All the economic fantasies that were built on borrowed money are now being exposed as paper frauds. So maybe someone made a decision that the idea of a safe war seemed better than facing unemployed voters at home. War can be good theater, the best theater in the world, if you're sure of the outcome. Maybe they figure Iraq will be a safe war. But I wouldn't bet a dime on it."

"We'll see in January."

"You know, Havlicek, since I've been over here I've come to see some things differently than I did before."

"How do you mean?"

"Where I grew up I had a chance to see the lives of people changed by radiation, some even die, like Phil. But Hanford is only a small part of the whole population and some people say it's nothing but an exception and it doesn't represent anything in the American culture. But here a whole country was exposed to something inhuman. At times it's easy to think of history as something impersonal and as something inevitable that can't be changed. But that's false. When you live here you begin to question the idea of history being inevitable. I knew, of course, there were American soldiers under General Patton here, but without actually living here and seeing real people, it was easy to

A HOME IN BOHEMIA 89

impersonalize it and to think of it as something historically inevitable. That blurs out the immorality of American politicians cutting a deal with a man like Stalin and for stopping Patton from going on to Prague and Berlin before the Russians. Maybe it was easy to divide up Europe on a map sitting in some air conditioned office in Washington, D.C. I suppose it's like war, if you never have to get close enough to it to see human faces then you can make it impersonal. People can make inhuman decisions if other people are reduced to only faceless numbers on a map. Someone can then make a decision to release radiation over innocent people or even give away a whole country, like Czechoslovakia, all in the name of some political policy. If you can impersonalize things enough, then any action, no matter how inhuman, can be done."

"Did the death of your brother start you thinking this way?"

Wilson studied the floor before he answered. "After Phil died I started thinking then how a man had a responsibility to change what he sees is wrong. Coming here and seeing faces every day in the streetcars and beer halls and cafes, I want to know how decisions were made that hurt so many innocent people. Because now I no longer believe what happened here after the war was inevitable or that it happened out of naivete. It was Roosevelt himself who said, *'Nothing in politics happens by accident.'* A student of mine brought me a new book about American soldiers in Plzen and it had a document written by an American Army Officer. I found a kind of poetry in it because his words were so simple and sincere."

Wilson reached up to his bookcase and removed a book and opened it.

17 July, 1945

To the Citizens of Bleistadt -

"During the period of our stay in your area to assist the Czechoslovak Republic in its reorganization, we have been unable to engage in social intercourse with you because of regulations imposed by higher authorities. However, we wish that such regulations had been different, because we wanted to know about you, and to be your friends. Please remember us kindly - we have attempted to conduct ourselves as soldiers of a democratic nation. In the rebirth of your Republic, may you be guided bye the principles of firmness, as well as by the principles of tolerance and charity."

    C.E. Gooding Lt. Colonel Commanding Hq.
    2nd Battalion infantry 79th Inf. Div.

"A student brought that to me because I've asked them to bring me any old photographs or records their grandparents might have of Americans. What happened here was different than what happened at Hanford because it changed the history of a whole country and because American officials collaborated with Stalin our history is connected to your history. Those who collaborated later claimed to be naive but it's false. Stalin had a known history, just as the dangers of radiation were well known before 1944. The suffering of innocent people everywhere will be meaningless if we don't change things."

"And what did you decide you should do to help change things?"

"I decided I had two choices. I could speak out against the old kind of thinking and risk alienating my colleagues and superiors or I could do nothing and lose my self-respect."

"What did you choose to do?"

"In the beginning I spoke out and made enemies and I was about to be transferred to a dead end job in my district when an economic slump hit the community and they suddenly had a chance to eliminate my job. After that I sort of retired."

"How do you mean?"

"When the economy recovered and my old job became available

A HOME IN BOHEMIA 91

I didn't apply for it but remained a substitute teacher, which meant I had no specific responsibilities, but I didn't have to lie to anyone either. I became a kind of non-person."

Havlicek smiled. "We know all about non-persons here, we turned not saying anything into an art because we learned the consequences of speaking out. But you're right, you lose your self-respect in silence. It makes you feel inhuman and that is why you see so many frozen faces in the streetcars and trolley busses. Just because the communists are out of power doesn't mean that these faces will change. The older people will never learn to take off the masks and only some of the people of my generation will learn to remove them. You must remember these masks were put on out of fear and once fear becomes a permanent part of someone's personality, it can't be rooted out overnight. A new personality for our country can only be made by those younger than us, much younger I'm afraid, by those who haven't been infected with fear."

"And what will this new Czechoslovakian personality be like? Will it be only a carbon copy of German things? They watch German television and German television seems to me too much like American television, a kind of jello where no matter how deep you dig you can never find a spine because there is none. Is this what the new Czech personality will be like, spineless?"

"Yes, I think it's inevitable that the new Czechoslovakia will become a clone of Western Europe, which has been influenced by American culture for the last forty-five years. It's inevitable because we now live in an electronic age, like it or not. My students listen to the same hard rock that teenagers listen to in Western Europe and our theaters are flooded with American films, as you know. The masses in our culture will come to look and think like the masses in the west. It's inevitable. But there are always individuals who will rise above the masses. I think Vaclav Havel is proof of that. And isn't our greatest responsibility to teach students to think clearly? Most won't learn, but some will and we must take hope in the few. Perhaps it seems like small hope, but

I can remember when there seemed no hope at all here. I'm curious, is there any reason beside your interest in history that you've asked your students to bring you old photographs of the American Army?"

Wilson smiled. "I find myself wanting to know if my father was here and what did he do here."

"Why does it matter to you, you said you no longer care about him?"

"I suppose it's only sentiment, but I wonder if perhaps he did something good or human or decent. Who knows, perhaps I can even find someone who remembers him, but I know it's probably pointless."

"Don't be so pessimistic."

"Well we have a saying, leopards don't change their spots. And even if he was here, and even if I find someone who knew him, probably the only thing they will remember is that he liked to drink and gamble and have a good time. It's a kind of fool's errand, a sentimental journey."

"Well I think it's always better to learn the truth, no matter how painful it might be."

"Do you really believe that?"

"Yes."

"Even if it means learning something bad about one of your own parents?"

"Yes, I'd rather have the truth."

"Then you're a bigger Greek than me."

"Maybe it's closer to the truth to say we have the same kind of blood."

Wilson laughed. "For you, I hope not."

"Maybe it's not as bad as you think."

"No, it's always worse than you think. You think things can't get any worse and you're wrong. Things can always get worse. Believe me, I know it."

Havlicek smiled. "Life is full of surprises."

Chapter 16

Wilson noticed her in one of the Monday afternoon staff meetings. He had no obligation to attend the meeting since he could not understand what was being said but he had a curiosity to learn whether the weekly staff meetings could generate the same kind of boredom in his new school as they did in American schools. It was also a good opportunity to count noses and see the faces of the whole school.

She was blond and sitting next to Petr, the oversized art teacher. Petr tried hard to fulfill the role of an art instructor, he let his whiskers grow to a stubble, but not a full beard, his clothing was always wrinkled as if he had slept in them and his hair was never combed.

Throughout the drone of the meeting she smiled at Wilson. He was sure he had not seen her before, he would have remembered her face. There was a trace of something Czech in her face. The eyes were hooded, the forehead rather high and broad and the mouth full. She was under thirty-five, Wilson speculated, although she had the kind of smooth skin that made a face look younger than it might have been. He thought she was appealing and decided to ask Petr after the meeting who she was and what she taught.

Wilson learned from Petr she was Dagmar Slavatova. She taught Physics and she was not married. Three days later he found her sitting in Petr's office. She looked gloomy, even morose. Wilson started to introduce himself.

"I know who you are," she interrupted in English before he could finish the sentence.

Looking into her eyes Wilson saw pain and felt awkward, her sadness was naked. He felt as if he had stumbled into someone undressing. "Can I help you?"

"No, no one can help me."

Wilson chewed at his lower lip trying to think of something to say. "If you would like to talk, I'm finished with my classes at three."

She looked up without making reply and Wilson seeing her up close noticed her mouth. It was a girlish mouth, but one that looked to him that could be tender at the right moment. Her eyes were girlish and old looking at the same time with the pain in them. Instinctively he felt he couldn't help with her pain; there was something self-inflicted about it. But he ignored his instinct in exchange for the satisfaction of trying to discover what her pain was about.

"Well, are you free today at three?"

"Yes, I'm free."

"Where would you like to meet?"

"At the front entrance."

She was waiting at the front entrance, still wearing the sad eyes. "How about some wine, there is a nice wine bar around the

corner," Wilson suggested.
She nodded.
"How long have you been teaching here?"
"Five years."
"Do you like it?" Wilson asked as they rounded the corner and approached the *vinarna*.
"No."
"What would you rather be doing?"
"I don't know."
"Do you have a boyfriend?"
"Yes."
"What does he do?"
"He is a doctor."
"Here in Plzen?"
"No, he lives in Prague."
"Move to Prague."
"I can't find a flat there."
Wilson studied her as he took his first drink of wine. There was something illogical about her. "Then move in with him."
"It's not possible."
Wilson nodded as if he understood.
"Where do you live in Plzen?"
"Under a bridge."
Wilson nodded. "Welcome home brother," he whispered and took a drink of wine.
"What did you say?"
"Nothing."
"It sounded interesting."
"It wasn't."
"What was it?"
"Nothing. What kind of hobbies do you have, you know for pleasure."
"Sex."
Wilson nodded. "That's a nice hobby. What part do you like best?"

"I like all of it."
"Tell me about your apartment."
"I told you, I live under a bridge."
"Do you have television under your bridge?"
"Yes."
"And telephone?"
"Yes."
"It must get cold there."
"Yes."
"Well you're always welcome to visit me in Lochotin."
"No, I don't think that's possible."
"Why not?"
"I would probably find another woman there getting warm."
"I don't have a girlfriend."
"I have heard you have plenty of girlfriends."
"You heard wrong, I don't have any girlfriends."
"I've heard students write love letters to you."
"You heard wrong again."
"No, I don't think so. One of my students is in love with you."
"Who?"
"One of the girls who wrote you a love letter."
"Who?"
"Sarka."
"Are you sure?"
"I know her mother, she is a friend of mine."
  Wilson nodded. He wasn't worried about the student. Young girls have illusions and they outgrow them. But the girl's mother troubled him. Wilson could feel something intense in the mother's eyes when she looked at him. And she already had a husband. She was trouble, not the daughter. Roman Havlicek was right, there seemed to be no secrets in their school. Maybe there were no secrets in Plzen.
  "She wants to be your daughter, so why don't you take care of her?"

"I'm very busy now and I haven't time to be a father to her or anyone else."
"You could telephone her."
"I don't have a telephone."
"You don't care about her - or her mother."
"I care a lot about her. She is one of my best students. And I like her mother, but she already has a husband."
"The problem is you have too many girlfriends."
"I told you, I don't have a girlfriend."
"Men like you always have girlfriends."
"What do you mean, men like me, you don't know what kind of man I am."
"Yes I do. You like to look at women and they like to look back at you."
"But I'm an old fashioned man, I look, but I stop at looking."
"Men are men. All look and all go further when they have a chance."
"You seem to know a lot about men."
"I know enough to know trouble when I see it, you're trouble."
"Why?"
"You know nothing about life in Czechoslovakia."
"I never said I did."
"You should learn before you mix yourself up with women."
"I'll remember your advice."
"No you won't."
"If someone wanted to send you a Christmas card, which bridge would they send it to?"
"They could send it to the school."
"I've lived under a bridge before."
"Have you?"
"Sure. Lots of them. I know all about living under bridges."
"Excuse me, I have to go home."
Wilson nodded and she was up out of her chair before he could pay the waiter. Outside he looked around for her. It had begun to

snow lightly in the early evening half light. He saw her from the backside walking away on Skroupova in the direction of Moskevska street. Her whole body seemed a picture of resignation, her head slumped looking at the ground, her stride shortened to a limp. His instinct became sure that he couldn't help her and he ought not to see her again. But he knew he would. The badly wounded had a certain appeal.

Chapter 17

"So how are things coming along with Martina Bellekova?" Jane asked without looking up from the class papers she was grading on her desk.

"What do you mean how are things coming, what things? There aren't any things coming with Martina Bellekova."

"I heard you took her to the movies, which film did you see?"

"This is the smaller town than I thought, who did you hear that from?"

"Oh, I don't remember where I heard it. But students go to the films too, Wilson, and you must remember that anything you do in Plzen is news. So which film did you see?"

"Cas Sluha."

"Did you like it?"

"Not much. I probably lost some of it because of the Czech, but even in English the idea of watching Yuppies climbing over each other to get to the top of the corporate ladder is stale stuff."

"How about Martina, did she like it?"

"I don't know. She's quiet."

"I've heard she is a strange woman."

"Just because you're quiet doesn't mean you're strange."

"Well, most women have married by the time they reach Martina's age."

"Obviously she hasn't found the right guy."

"Maybe she isn't looking for the right guy, Wilson."

Wilson turned to look at Jane Tozantova. "What are you trying to say, that she's a lesbian? Come on, I guess I would know one when I see one."

"Don't be so touchy. How would you know?"
"Believe me I would know."
"How?"
"Dammit, I would know. Believe me."
"Take it easy. Maybe you're right. Maybe Martina Bellekova hasn't found the right guy. Maybe you're the right guy."
"I doubt it. She's a nice woman and that's all there is to it."
"Of course. And how are things coming along with Dagmar?"
"Stuff it!"
"Such language, Wilson."
"There aren't any things with Dagmar Slavatova. We had a glass of wine. That's it."
"She isn't liked by her students, you know. They hate her."
"So what?"
"So they know something about her. She isn't liked by other teachers either."
"I don't give a damn about what the other teachers like."
"Everyone says she is a strange woman."
"Maybe I like strange women."
"Somebody said she is a nymphomaniac!"
"If she is she is probably having more fun than anybody in this school and probably the person who started that rumor is both unmarried and homely."
"Have you ever considered the possibility, Wilson, that you have a talent to find difficult and strange women? I'll bet your women in America were also difficult."

Wilson tapped his ballpoint pen against the top of his desk.

"Maybe the reason you're attracted to difficult and strange women is because you're also difficult and strange."
"Tozantova maybe the truth is that I like interesting women who live independent lives because I'm an independent and, possibly, even an interesting man."
"But what were the women like who you knew in America?"
"They were interesting, Tozantova, very interesting."

"Yes, I imagine so. And very difficult too."
"Life is difficult."
"Yes, especially in Czechoslovakia. So one need not look for more difficulty, should they?"
"No, they shouldn't."
"Then why do you do it, Wilson?"
"I don't, but sometimes one finds people who need some help and so we have to give them a hand."
"Don't kid yourself, the kind of women you know are looking for more than a hand."
"I can take care of myself."
"Yes, I imagine in games like basketball you are primitive enough to, as you say, protect your territory. But in the game we're talking about I think you lack the instinct to protect yourself. It's strange, Wilson, how you can be so primitive in one thing and so naive in another."
"The truth is, Tozantova, I don't think there is a woman in Plzen who you would approve of if I was interested in her."
"Oh no, that's not true. There are lots of women who I approve of, I just think it's interesting how you have a talent to find difficult and strange women from among all the normal ones."
"I suppose that is a matter of opinion. No doubt you would approve of anyone who is dull and orthodox."
"Not at all."
"Yes, that's it, you approve of dull women and the orthodox and I have an allergy to everything dull."
"You have a talent for trouble, Wilson, like a dog chases a cat, and I'll bet if I met some of your women in America all I would find is trouble. Tell me I'm wrong."
"You're wrong."
Jane Tozantova laughed. "You're hopeless, David. You can't fool me. Tell me the name of one normal woman you've been involved with since you've been divorced?"
"I don't discuss my relationships, it violates a gentleman's

ethics."

"Being a gentleman has nothing to do with you, so come on, tell me the name of one normal woman you've known since you've been divorced."

"Believe it or not I've known plenty of normal women."

"I don't believe it. I'll bet you a hundred korun that by February this office will be filled with so much gloom and trouble you can cut it with a knife."

"Sure, what's a hundred *korun*. I could always use some extra cash."

"Bet me?"

"Sure."

"By the way there is some mail for you I set next to the typewriter."

"Thanks," Wilson said as Jane left the office. One letter was in a pink envelope without a stamp, probably from a student. Dammit, Wilson thought, Jane was probably there when someone brought it. Don't students know when they write these letters it makes rumors and troubles. If God was so smart why did he make seventeen year old girls with the bodies of grown women, but without any sense? Wilson flipped the pink envelope into a desk drawer without opening it.

The other letter had a strange looking stamp on it and was forwarded from his old address at home. It came from Russia. Who could be writing him from Russia? He didn't know anyone in Russia. He tore the seal of the letter open and skipped to the bottom of the page to read the signature. Yes, he did know someone in Moscow, a teacher who came to his old school for one year on an exchange program. She wrote she was going to Holland for an international conference of Teachers for Peace and she had heard from another teacher at Hanford that he was in Czechoslovakia, she would be happy to detour for a visit on her journey, if he was interested? Why not, Wilson thought. He smiled thinking how it would annoy Jane if she heard he had a female visitor for Christmas from Russia. On the other hand it annoyed him that so many people seemed to know details about his personal life and Wilson resolved that his private life was going to become private. Totally private.

Chapter 18

It's a dangerous thing you're doing, Wilson thought as he sat in his office reading the letter which came in the pink envelope several days earlier from one of his students. You can't stop teenage girls from having illusions. And you can't be all things to all people, it can only end up badly if you encourage it. It was a stupid thing to do to try and wash one woman out of your system by getting involved with another woman. It was stupid and wrong.

You'd tried it before, in Portland, after Pat. It didn't work then and it won't work now. The problem then was you were too young to know it could not work and too proud to simply accept losing until time washed out the pain. You were too young and too proud to accept it gracefully and you used other people to help you. But it ended badly because it involved other people wrongly and brought them needless suffering to go along with your own suffering.

You thought you had grown stronger as you grew older and the long runs through the desert on white-hot days as well as running on cold winter days had hardened something inside you to ward off any pain from things like women. But it was only illusion. Nothing helped a man to avoid pain, such as the pain a woman's face and voice could create. Like the pain Martina Bellekova makes. You could never predict where you'd meet a painful face or voice or what it could look or sound like. But after you met the wrong face or voice, no matter how strong you thought you were, you were wrong because a face or voice could come alive in the quiet of the night or in the middle of the day or even when you were with another woman. And time did not always wash a woman out of your system, Wilson learned, for what you once loved in a woman's face or voice at twenty you could still love in another woman at thirty or forty, it didn't matter if her language or her country was different than the woman in your past.

But it was not only stupid but cowardly to mix another woman into your life when you were suffering. Cowardly because a woman had a right to know if you loved the idea of another woman. There are rights in everything, even in love and war. You would not expect a man to buy a house or car without knowing its history. And a woman had a right to know if a man had mortgaged his heart to another woman. That's an investment right of a woman. The problem is you can't explain to any other person about what you feel. Martina Bellekova made the problem worse by placing a barrier between you and her that stopped a relationship from developing or allowing it to die a natural death that comes when feelings between a man and woman lack the needed chemistry. The barrier he felt between them had the feel of something unnatural and cut against him until something felt raw inside.

Wilson felt resentment and instinctively tried to harden his feelings against her. There was nothing else to do, he reasoned. Still, the decent thing to do was to keep away from other women until you had suffered a woman out of your system. The problem was, you'd learned, staying away from other women solved nothing. You learned nothing from it and afterward there was no new wisdom. It did not make you feel better about life or feel more human or heroic. In fact, it made a desert inside you at the place where normal feelings are born and develop into things good or bad. It mutated something inside you. Then when you experienced new things, where you used to feel something, there was nothing but desert, not compassion or anger or wonder or desire. Nothing but nothing. It was as if someone had loosened the strings of a violin or guitar and when a moment arrived to strike a note there was only silence. The mind knew from experience what to do, but inside something had became warped from forced isolation until it was useless.

Self-exile was futile because it solved nothing and in fact killed something necessary in people. Why was it, Wilson wondered, that all the great books, including the Bible, and all the great philosophers, such as Plato, had so little or nothing to say about the struggles a man has with a woman? Because Wilson admitted, with a smile, they knew nothing about it. Ecclesiastes would only say, "A man will endure every other kind of pain before he suffers the pain of love."

Wilson sat as his desk taping a corner of the pink envelope against his desk top. Finally he threw it impatiently back into the drawer. Even King Solomon knew there was no cure for the kind of fate he was struggling against. Once it came you could suffer in exile or you could suffer in the arms of a stranger. It made no difference, the results always came out the same.

Wilson bit his lip and tilted his head ever so slightly as he thought about Martina Bellekova.

Chapter 19

He had never seen such sadness in a woman's face. It wasn't the sharp acid kind of sadness that fills a face with bitterness, but rather a kind of elegant sadness a woman can wear with the same dignity as a new sweater or jacket. Wilson stole glances at her and studied her when he could from over the shoulder of a passenger standing beside him on the streetcar. He would not have seen her at all if he had not forgotten some school papers on his kitchen table and had to jump a streetcar from school to return to his flat, grab the papers on the run, and jump the first streetcar to make it to class on time.

Her sadness captured him and he decided he must meet her, if there was a chance of it. He couldn't guess her age, but decided that she was probably not as old as her face made her appear to be. It was the shape of her face that hid her age. It reminded him of the face of a movie actress out of the past. Somehow it seemed she had jumped out of an old black and white film and been transported into the present. It seemed to him that she must have witnessed something out of the past that was too sad to leave behind and it stayed in her eyes. Wilson hoped she would get off the streetcar at his stop and that he could invent some means to speak to her. As the streetcar braked to a halt, rocking passengers forward as they hung from the handgrips, she stood at his stop and departed so that she did not lurch forward as the other passengers did and stepped off the steps without looking right or left, but with the same dignified sadness as she had stared out the window.

There was a thin crust of snow on the ground and Wilson opened up his stride slightly to pull even with her. But as he walked beside her his mind fumbled for words. He stole a glance at her, but she stared straight ahead without a change of expression.

"Pardon me," Wilson managed.

She glanced at him.

"Can you speak English or German?"

"Yes," she answered, "some English."

"I think you're very pretty."

She glanced at him, as if not understanding or caring to.

"I saw you on the streetcar."

"Are you from England?"

"No, I'm an American."

Wilson thought he detected a spark of interest or at least a change of expression in her eyes. "What are you doing in Plzen?"

"I teach English at the *gymnazium*," Wilson said with a nod toward his school across the street behind the economy school.

Her face returned to the same impenetrable mask and Wilson felt he had reached a wall and that she was telling him with silence their conversation was over.

"Is there a telephone number where I could call you?"

"Yes. Would you prefer my work number or home number?"

"Both," Wilson said deciding to press his luck.

Without another word she opened her purse and removed a small note pad and hastily wrote out two numbers. "Would you like to know my name too?"

"Yes, excuse me."

"I assume you have a name too?" she said while writing her name below the numbers.

"I'm David Wilson."

"My name is Jitka Visnekova."

"When could I call you?"

"Anytime you wish, but if you telephone me at home a teenage girl will answer the phone, she speaks German but no English, that's my daughter."

Wilson managed a smile and nodded and crossed the street

toward his school.

After school he met her for coffee, Wilson learned she was his neighbor and lived only two tram stations up the street from him in Lochotin. When she invited him to her flat for dinner he was surprised to find her teen-age daughter had a face nearly identical to the mother's, but without any sadness in it her face struck him as completely different. She was a normal teen-age girl full of laughter and nervous energy just as any of his students. Like her mother, she was slender and tall. There was also a cat and a dog in the household. Everything about the family seemed normal, except there was no man in it and the feeling of sadness from a past life hung in the air.

She was from a city in Moravia, she told him after super, as they sat in her living room drinking coffee and watching televi- sion. She was a student in Prague when she met the man she later married. He was a successful lawyer some fifteen years older than her. Then came the Prague spring of 1968 and she had in her enthusiasm signed some student petitions against the communist government. After the Russian invasion she found herself expelled from the university and she made another harsh discovery: her father wasn't just a communist but a member of the secret police. He refused to help her in any way when he learned of her political opinions.

She became pregnant by the lawyer and got married. Her husband was sent to Plzen by his employer. The marriage was short and bitter. Without supplying details she spoke of her ex-husband as only a ruthless man. She divorced him and went to work as a secretary for Skoda in Plzen and remained there with her infant daughter. Wilson expected her history to include a second husband but there was no mention of one.

An hour or so after her daughter had come to say good night and announce she was going to bed, Jitka Visnekova turned to Wilson and whispered, "We can sleep here or in my bedroom where it is more comfortable, but it is next to my daughter's bedroom and we must be very quiet. What do you prefer?"

"I'll try to be very quiet," Wilson whispered and followed her into the darkness.

Chapter 20

Wilson shook himself out of his sleep and silenced his alarm clock by pushing the alarm button off and rolled into a sitting position. It felt unnatural to be up so early and even the idea of coffee seemed out of place. The only thing which made any sense to his fogged brain was to crawl back under the blanket and sleep. But he knew without having to think that he had to catch a train to Prague and be there by five to meet Zoya's train from Moscow. He knew it without thinking and fought off the impulse to reset the alarm clock and milk some more sleep out of the darkness.

He also knew there were but two streetcars every hour after midnight and if he missed the first the second might not get him to the train station on time. So he staggered up and boiled water for coffee and dressed. Then with his coffee in a plastic cup in one hand and his briefcase in the other he rode the elevator down to the ground floor and pushed out into the freezing darkness.

Zoya hadn't changed, he thought, when he first saw her; heavy breasted, thin legs and narrow hips, always a curious combination in a woman. Wilson smiled warmly as she walked toward him from her coach, as much to mask his own uneasiness with the situation as to greet her. He had not actually taken her out when Zoya had taught at Hanford, they had merely shared lunch hour conversations at school. He had never given it a second thought that she always sat down next to him in the lunch room if they happened to have the same lunch schedule. Nor had he given it much thought that she wrote him a warm good bye letter at the end of the school year and asked him to write to her in Moscow. The truth was he had never had any desire to start a relationship with her when she was in America.

Riding the train into Prague he tried to decide upon some kind of attitude to employ during her visit. Cordial but firm about it being only a friendly visit or simply to let things go where they did spontaneously. But Wilson couldn't decide upon an attitude and truthfully he didn't care. It seemed to make no difference in the scheme of anything that someone from Russia was visiting him. It was just one more illogical event to life in Plzen.

In the warmth of the train back to Plzen Zoya seemed happy to see him and Wilson struggled to remember if there was something he had said or done when he knew her at Hanford to give her the idea there was a potential for a relationship. He could remember nothing in particular. The words of Jane Tozantova returned, "Have you ever considered the possibility, Wilson, that you have a talent to find difficult and strange women....Maybe the reason you are attracted to difficult and strange women is because you yourself are difficult and strange."

Thinking of Jane's words Wilson felt annoyed. He glanced down at Zoya's face, which rested on his right shoulder where she had fallen asleep. Was she a difficult and strange woman? She seemed to him to be normal.

"Do you remember some of the things we talked about back in the States?" Wilson asked her as they sat at his kitchen table in the early evening drinking some *Tokajsky,* after supper.

She smiled. "How do you mean, which kind of things?"

"I've been trying to think about what we talked about and it seems unclear now, like it happened in another life."

"I remember one day we talked about something that stands out from the others. It was spring time and sunny and we ate lunch together out on the front lawn of the school. It was not only sunny but warm and the air had that wonderful desert dryness in it. We sat on the lawn and talked about the novel *Anna Karenina.* I'd never met anyone in America who understood Russian feelings in that book as you did. And I also remember we talked about

Turgenev's *First Love*. You seemed to admire the sentiment of it as I do and I felt from that time you were different than other Americans I met."

"Maybe you were mistaken."

"About what?"

"About me, maybe I'm no different than other Americans."

"No, I'm sure of it."

"Is that good or bad?"

"I think it's good because it means to me you feel deeply about life, maybe as deep as an artist."

Wilson laughed. "I think maybe you have the wrong idea about me."

"Are you embarrassed to be compared to an artist?"

Wilson frowned. "What do you know about artists?"

"Have you ever wondered how some dissidents survived during the Bhreznev years after they were thrown out of their jobs? Here is how some survived. At the technical institute where I work we have a budget and in this budget there is always money for guest lectures. So we would pay some dissidents big fees and stipends to come and lecture at our institute - a kind of passive resistance," she exclaimed by laughing softly.

"I got to know many artists through our institute. I found one thing almost all had in common, an intense feeling about life. It's something I never met in anyone in America, until I met you. That's what I meant."

"Where do you think this intensity comes from?"

"From suffering."

"Suffering?"

"Yes, Bhreznev wasn't Stalin, but there was still plenty of suffering. People still went to jail or would find themselves in some mental asylum for saying the wrong thing, for questioning, and for many other things. I felt that you had suffered some kind of loss in life, am I right?"

Wilson hesitated. "Maybe."

"I'm quite sure of it, it's made you think carefully about things most people avoid thinking about. Not Americans anyway."

Wilson finished his wine and poured himself another glass. "I'm not so sure it's good to think too carefully about life."

"Why not?"

"You learn more than you should."

"You think there's a limit on how much someone should learn about life?"

Wilson smiled and bit his lip. "Solzhenitsyn told a graduating class at Harvard, *'Truth is invariably bitter.'* Too much truth can turn someone bitter."

"Maybe. But I want to learn all I can. And I doubt there's much in life we can avoid. The dissidents I met in Moscow are that way because it's their nature. It's the nature of a person that leads him in one direction or the other, so I wasn't surprised to hear from someone that you'd come to Czechoslovakia."

"But I'm surprised to be here."

"Not me, I couldn't imagine you staying at Hanford. It's not your nature to remain in such a place."

"What do you mean, such a place?"

"It's too static, too passive, too orthodox. Your nature is the opposite, you know. You're more primitive and instinctive. It seems to me you're the kind of person who has to be where there is a challenge, something to throw yourself at."

"I'm sleepy," Wilson said. "I have two beds, the one in the bedroom and the couch you're sitting on, it unfolds into a bed. Take your pick."

Zoya smiled and gazed into Wilson's eyes. "I want the one you're sleeping in."

Wilson nodded. "You're a difficult woman, all right."

"All interesting women are difficult and I'm very difficult and interesting."

Wilson nodded.

Chapter 21

Havlicek broke into a smile when he saw Wilson walk through his office doorway. "Happy New Year, if you didn't come to see me today then I was going down to see you. How was your Christmas vacation in old Bohemia?"
"Busy," Wilson answered.
"How about a cup of coffee?"
"Fine, if you've got something besides sugar to put in it."
"No problem, sit down."
Instead Wilson circled Havlicek's desk and stood at the window looking over Petakova street at the steeple of the catholic church stuck above the other roof tops. "I like these old buildings, I feel something human in them that's good. I can't feel it in the modern architecture, do you know what I mean?"
"Sure," Havlicek said. "When I look at modern buildings I feel something that is sterile, but when I look at the old buildings I feel something human. It's easy to imagine interesting stories and people in the old buildings."
"Why is it, Havlicek," Wilson began without turning to look at his friend, "that all the wise men of the ages never write anything wise about women?"
Havlicek smiled as he poured rum into their steaming coffee and stirred in sugar. "You ask the unanswerable question. Wise men write about the origin of the universe, the nature of God and the meaning of good and evil, but they are silent when it comes to the one subject men need wisdom about, the nature of women."
"Oh, hell," Wilson said turning and sitting down in a heap, "every so-called philosopher and imbecile writer since Plato has

had something to say about women, but it's all worthless. Nothing but junk. And there is even more nonsense written about love. And nothing intelligent ever written about sex."

"You sound like a man in love."

"Crap. I'm not in love with anyone."

"So you came to tell me you're not in love with anyone," Havlicek said with a smile.

Wilson took a drink of his coffee and savored the rum flavor. "It seems odd to me that we're asked to believe all kinds of things about the most distant things in the universe, asked to believe the most unlikely things about religion, but when we need truth about the things we must deal with everyday in our lives, neither science or religion has any answers...."

"You're speaking about women, of course?"

Wilson continued as if he had not heard Roman Havlicek's comment. "Plato had something to say about damn near everything, but we don't know whether he was ever married or had a mistress or had his heart broken by some Greek woman. Why don't we know that? How can we trust a man to tell us how to live when we don't know whether the guy could manage his own life any better than the average idiot?"

"If you've come to me to argue with, you've come to the wrong man. I've had my own misfortunes with women."

"I don't want to argue, I'd just like some answers."

Havlicek took a drink of his rum and coffee and smiled at Wilson.

"What are you smiling at?"

"You. I knew it was only a matter of time before things started to happen."

"Nothing has happened."

"I hear you and Dagmar are - "

"Nothing is happening with Dagmar."

"With Dagmar something is always happening."

"Not with me. She belongs on a funny farm."

"What is a funny farm?"
"It's a rest home for head cases."
"Lots of people say that's where she belongs and if you hang around with her enough, things will happen."
"My life is complicated enough that I don't need any head cases in it."
"What's complicating your life, tell me her name?"
"That has nothing to do with what I'm talking about."
"What is it that has to do with anything?"
"The thing is," Wilson began, "I'm a very basic kind of man, yet my life seems too often to become involved with people who are complicated and then people accuse me of being like them."
"I can't imagine someone thinking you're a complicated man," Havlicek remarked lightly.
"Go to hell, what else have you got in your medicine cabinet for emergencies?"
"Vodka, I always keep vodka handy for a medical emergency."
Wilson nodded and Havlicek poured them each a shot glass of vodka. "Do I know this lucky Czech woman who you are not in love with?"
Wilson took a drink of vodka and scowled at Havlicek. "The thing is my life has gotten messy lately. I'm doing things that I've never done before and which I don't believe in. Maybe I even hate them."
"Such as?"
Wilson turned his glass around in his fingers and studied it. "I've slept with women lately that I don't care about."
"You've never done that in America?"
"I was young then and I didn't know any better. Now I know better."
"So why are you doing it?"
"I'm trying to forget someone."
"Why?"
"Because she doesn't care about me, I care about her but she

doesn't care about me."
"What's her name?"
"Never mind."
"Do I know her?"
Wilson ignored the question. "But the harder I try to forget her it seems the more I think about her. And I feel like a criminal for being involved with other women, but I know from experience it doesn't matter. I used to think I was strong enough to fight my way through these kinds of things, but I learned that's not true either."
"You're sure this woman doesn't care about you?"
Wilson smiled. "I'm not sure of anything anymore. Maybe she doesn't even like men, maybe she likes women."
"Wouldn't you know if she did?"
"I used to think I would."
"I was in love with a woman once for six years. I wanted to marry her. But it didn't work out. So I tried being with other women, even sleeping with some, but it didn't help me either. I didn't think I was ever going to get over her. Maybe I never have. Even today if I happen to walk by her home I feel strange inside and if I happen to be in a cafe or restaurant where we once were at I catch myself glancing at the table where we sat, as if somehow she would materialize. I learned nothing about the most fundamental aspect of existence: the need for another human being. Even after a love affair is dead and cold in the ground, it can spring to life again in the body of another person and you experience the old pain all over again. I've seen sides of this woman in other women and felt the old love tear into my flesh. It's a thousand times more complex than physics and as long as man exists I doubt he'll ever understand it. So it doesn't surprise me that you've tried to escape in the arms of another woman, many have tried that, including me."
"The worst part is I feel dead afterward. I feel I've violated some law but I can't understand it. I feel as if I've destroyed some part

of myself and yet I've learned from experience that too much solitude also ends up destroying some part of myself. So you lose either way and you can't explain it to anyone. You think you can because you believe there must be words for everything that exists. But you learn that isn't true either, you learn that there are things there are no words for and it separates you from the rest of the world."

Chapter 22

Wilson left Havlicek's office and walked down the three flights of stairs, his right knee was sore from playing basketball the night before. At the school entrance the concierge came out and handed him a letter. He glanced at it and saw the Dutch stamps and the handwriting of Zoya. He stuck it in his jacket pocket and walked around the school to the gril, ordered a beer and opened the letter It was typed on stationary with a hotel logo at the top.

       Amsterdam
       3 January, 1991

Dear David:
    It was a long ride on the train, but it gave me the time I needed to think in solitude.
    Growing up in Russia one learns there is less to be certain of in life and one must learn how to think more clearly at a younger age than in other countries. One must learn, for example, how to judge another person's character. For in times past, and to a lesser degree now, one had to select their friends wisely for the wrong friend could destroy you. Indeed merely expressing the wrong opinion to the wrong person could destroy you.
    You learned how to evaluate people. I know this much about you, you need a certain order in your life. I know that you were alienated by life in America, most likely because of the superficiality.
    Most people in Western countries never understand the dangers of superficial life because they neither understand its full dangers

or where its origins come from. In Russia we understand it better.

For having to live an existence under slogans that are lies one sees where superficiality ends when carried far enough. Superficiality can only breed in a society that has grown too lazy or too fearful to think clearly so they adapt language and habits which blur out reality. Bad music is just one example. Creating good music requires talent and genuine feeling. Making bad music requires neither talent or genuine feeling.

The music one hears most often in America is endless repetitions of one line or even one word. It is the kind of music teen-agers listen to for hours. But American television seems built around the same laziness and lack of genuine feelings. One sees over and over the endless detective shows and so-called comedies in which people laugh at idiotic remarks. That mentality spills over into political life as well. All is superficial. Empty slogans dominate so an idiot can become elected merely by repeating slogans modeled for television. And so very often in America real idiots become elected.

For a person who thinks deeply about life, how many hours of exposure to superficiality can they endure before they are alienated down to their roots?

But I found when I criticized superficial life in America I was very often greeted with a kind of stunned silence, as if something larger was being criticized. It is almost as if the *"American way of life,"* is thought to have some kind of legal protection for the thoughtlessness and idiocy one witnesses in daily life. So anyone who criticizes it is considered to be against something American, that then identifies the critic as anti-American!

But where is it written that freedom must include stupidity? Can't one live freely and intelligently at the same time? I think so.

I think you do too. Somewhere one must find a life where there is the right balance of social order combined with intelligence and there will find beauty. But does such a place exist and can it exist in modern life?

It's difficult now for me to imagine you staying long in Czechoslovakia for you seem to me a kind of refugee out of the past. I don't know where men like you belong. For those who reject the superficial order of modern life instinctively sink their roots deeper and deeper into the ground in search of spiritual nourishment, they are doomed to find more conflict not less. For modern life is geared to speed not thoughtfulness. The result is superficiality increases and sincerity of thought decreases. To resist the grinding of these gears will bring only conflict - and disappointment.

Changes will flow into places like Bohemia from the West where traces of the old life were able to survive under communism. For in trying to stamp men's minds with Leninist dogma and erase the old patterns of personal thinking, communism offered nothing to tempt men out of old habits - even fear has limits. And dogma of any kind becomes a kind of target, as the Puritans learned when they failed to eliminate personal instincts about sex.

But the Western culture of materialism, instant pleasure and "social correctness," which opens the doors to the first two, will succeed where communism failed. When communists censored books they only made them more popular and valuable to read, but video games, VCRs and best seller books, will eliminate the desire to read literature in the numbers that communists could only envy.

To openly resist this trend will only earn you veiled contempt and the reputation of a rogue. I know, dear, because sometimes I lunched in the teacher's lounge at Hanford and the first time I innocently brought up your name in conversation I felt a chill and a hush, as if everyone within ear shot caught their breath at the same time. Glances were exchanged. So I set about playing detective to discover what your crime was.

There was no crime, of course. You simply expressed opinions that conflicted with what made people comfortable. You failed to eat with teachers and engage in their chit chat. Keeping to yourself is also outside of social correctness! And I learned about the death

A HOME IN BOHEMIA   123

of your brother, who everyone agreed was a "great guy." It was as if by making a point of agreeing your brother was a good guy, it justified them thinking you were a rogue. It amused me and made me want to know you more. For the most interesting people I knew in Moscow were the dissidents and I recognized your "crimes" were the same as theirs.

So where will you go? Back to Hanford to become a kind of desert rat? It seems to me you are too spirited for the role of a monk or a exile.

Will you meet some Bohemian woman and make a life in the old world? Somehow I can't imagine it. To fit in anywhere today and find a niche you'd have to sacrifice your own nature. I think you know already these words from Pericles,

"The Athenians are lovers of beauty without having lost the taste for simplicity, and lovers of wisdom without loss of manly vigor."

Since your instinct is for wisdom, you hate what is superficial and since your idea of what is manly won't allow you to hide behind silence, you can't blend in with the herd any easier in Bohemia than you could at Hanford.

So where will you go? Will you keep me informed of where you are? Do you resent me for spying on you at Hanford? Is this letter too grim? Too honest?

There are always possibilities in life that none of us can see in the future. The religious call it grace. The secular call it good luck.

I've learned only that life is enriched by time spent with persons strong enough to seek truth and gentle enough to give without asking for anything back. We call these good memories. So I'm richer today than before I came to Bohemia. Whatever the future, don't forget the words of Turgenev in *First Love* that we talked about out in the desert that spring day. Hold those words close to your heart. Maybe they can be the means of saving you when you are lost.

Love Zoya

124 A HOME IN BOHEMIA

Wilson folded the letter, but to be honest he couldn't remember the words of Turgenev she said they talked about. That day in the desert seemed to have happened a long time ago, almost another life ago. And the idea that the words of Turgenev, or anyone else, could be the means of saving him seemed a kind of fantasy.

Chapter 23

Wilson folded the letter thoughtfully and slid it back into its envelope. She was wrong, he thought. She was wrong about thinking he could not find some happiness in Bohemia. No one can be sure where a man can or can't be happy. Life can't be so concrete. It was true after his first look at Plzen he felt only regret. But month by month the regret declined.

The more he had walked the streets of Plzen the more the regret thinned out. Yes, Plzen was a smokestack city like some of the dark cities he had seen once driving through the Allegheny Valley region of Pennsylvania and West Virginia, where smoke from steel mills had turned the brick faced buildings the same grey-black of the buildings in Plzen. And it was true that on a day when clouds hung low and hid the green hills beyond the city from the sun, one did feel oppressed by the greyness of Plzen.

But as Havlicek had said; when he looked at the old buildings with murals painted on the belfries and facades so finely constructed, he could not help from thinking of the lives that had once existed inside those houses. Wilson had come to believe that people who would go to such trouble to construct beautiful things to the eye must have had a rich spirit. Most of the buildings, he noted by the dates of construction hewn into the stone faces, were built around the turn of the century, but he argued that if the spirit for beauty once existed in Bohemia, then there must still be traces of it alive to be woken up after nearly a century of slumber.

It was true that it would take years for the smoke stacks of Plzen to be fitted with emission controls to filter out the poisons in the air and to restore the old buildings to their glory. But it could be done. Wilson's students also helped thin out the regret. His best students were as good as any students he had known in America. He reasoned that if his students were good then they came from good backgrounds. There had to be something good in Bohemians, even after the systematic destruction of their culture, first by the Habsburgs, then the Nazis, then by the communists.

It wasn't just the pleasure of the old buildings or his students, Zoya was too pessimistic about the idea of happiness with a Czech woman. It was complicated so you couldn't blame her for her pessimism - Plato didn't seem to know much about it either. Maybe there was a hundred, maybe even two hundred, women in Plzen he could find some happiness with, maybe not forever, but what lasts forever anyway? Maybe Zoya, being a woman, was thinking of something larger than happiness, like love? But how many people have you known or ever heard about who were still in love after they had been married for a year or two? They were either happy enough to stay married or they became divorced. The truth was lots of people stayed married even if they were not happy because they were either too lazy or too timid to face life alone.

But Zoya didn't write about the one thing he'd learned long before coming to Plzen; a woman even if she couldn't make a man happy could damn sure make him unhappy and even miserable. So miserable he'd try to escape his misery by giving up his job and flee. Wilson had known a number of men who had tried to escape their misery brought about by a woman by moving to another city or even state.

A Bohemian woman or a woman anywhere else could destroy a man's chances for happiness. And it didn't have to be a beauty either. All it had to be was the wrong face or voice and a man could find himself in a black hole.

It could be Martina Bellekova.

Zoya hadn't any idea about Martina. You couldn't tell her, of course, any more than you could tell Roman Havlicek. There just wasn't any words for it. You were right when you told Havlicek the lack of words to explain it separated a man from the rest of the world.

Havlicek knew about that black hole. He knew it from experience. He admitted it when he said even today if he walked by her house he felt strange or went into a restaurant they used to visit he felt spooked. And he brought up something else that could ruin a man's happiness. An old love could come alive in another woman. Havlicek said an old love could spring to life again in the form of another woman and tear into your flesh.

Havlicek knew all right. Maybe Martina was only a reminder of someone from the past? Wilson took a drink of beer and shook his head. He remembered an experience he had the night before on a streetcar going home. He saw a young girl no more than ten or eleven, maybe younger, with a face and smile so gentle yet so intelligent that his heart felt like stopping. She had dark hair that was pulled back and clipped with barrettes. Her dark eyes were the happiest eyes he had ever seen. She wore a school uniform with red stockings and carried a school work box. When she got off the streetcar, one stop before his stop, a loneliness swept over him so sharp and deep he felt a touch of dizziness.

It had caught him with such surprise that he stumbled off the streetcar uncertain of himself. There were faces, he thought once again, that have some message in them that communicates something deeper than words.

It seemed to Wilson the one thing that caused more people more unhappiness and misery was something no one understood or wrote about intelligently. They didn't know where it came from or where it went or even if it really existed. All they knew for sure is that some poor stiffs jump off buildings and bridges because of it, some take poisons and some ruin their livers drinking bad booze because of it.

The guy who wrote everybody makes a fool of themselves sometime over somebody, probably got it right. So you had better not kid yourself, brother, it can happen to you too. It hasn't yet, but don't think you're too tough to avoid it. This has nothing to do with toughness or what it takes to run through the desert when the temperature is a hundred. This is about something no one understands and never has understood and never will understand.

It was probably only a matter of time before you made a fool of yourself and maybe you're overdue. Maybe your time just came up and it happens to be in a place called Bohemia. Making a fool of yourself over a woman is probably no worse than getting knocked silly in a boxing ring or on a football field. Maybe it's like some boxers say after they've been knocked out: it was so painless they didn't remember the punch.

Wilson finished his beer and took a deep breath. He shook his head again and bit his lower lip. This isn't like boxing at all. When a man cares deeply about a woman and something goes wrong the hurt can last a lifetime - and you remember the hurt and never do forget it.

But you're still a son of a bitch for involving anyone else with your misery. A gutless son of a bitch.

Chapter 24

Even with the help of a magnifying glass Wilson could not find what he hoped for. The old black and white photographs of American soldiers in Bohemia were too often poorly reproduced to reveal distinct faces. The uniforms were different than the soldiers of his generation; the shirts and jackets had no name tags. Another problem was that nearly every soldier wore a combat helmet or liner and trying to imagine what a man looked like at twenty-five and with his head covered complicated an already difficult job.

Despite his discouragement, he kept inspecting hundreds of old photographs that added more doubt. At times his hopes would soar when he found a soldier of about the right height, about the right body build, but whose face was half-hidden under a shadow or distorted by a combat helmet or the photograph was such poor quality that the soldier seemed to change from one shape to another before his eyes as a cloud can change shape from moment to moment in the sky.

Discouraged after weeks of studying old photographs and memorabilia, such as old school registers, he was at length forced to the conclusion he would have to search in Plzen for someone who had actually known Harry Wilson. It was a long shot, he conceded, like finding a needle in a haystack. He would need some luck or some help. He remembered Father Sedlacek's comment of repeating the old proverb that when God closes a door he sometimes opens a window. David Wilson smiled, good luck, brother.

Wilson followed Havlicek to the pub located on a side street near his school. Inside it was poorly lit and had dirty walls. The table cloth at the table they sat at was dirty and soiled. They ordered beer. "You think this guy might have known my father?"

Havlicek smiled. "I only said he was here then and knew plenty of American soldiers and I've never known him to make up anything. He's a serious man."

Wilson glanced at his watch.

"Relax, he'll come."

Wilson watched a man come through the door, look around the pub and walk toward their table. *"Dobre den."* Havlicek said and they shook hands. Wilson stood and held out his hand to Mr. Flak.

"I"m pleased to meet you," Flak said in English without an accent. "It's been a long time since I've met an American."

"I've been told you were here the day the American soldiers arrived."

"I remember it very clearly. It was early in the morning and I heard something like a rumbling and my first thought was that it was another bombing of the Skoda plant. Most of us were no longer working because of the damage at the plant by the bombings. There was a terrible incident at the Hotel Continental, maybe you know about it? Many people used the hotel's basement as a bomb shelter because it was considered to be such a strong structure. But one bomb came through a skylight and penetrated into the basement killing and injuring a great number of people. Later after the war was over the communists used this incident for propaganda purposes because everybody in Plzen knew these bombings were too late to be of any practical purpose. So the first thing I thought that morning was that there was another American bombing raid. I remember that morning clearly."

Looking at Mr. Flak and hearing his voice Wilson believed him. He had expected something else. Havlicek had told him that Mr. Flak had spent many years in prison under the communists and he expected a man with less vigor in his voice and appearance. But clearly Mr. Flak was an unbroken man.

A HOME IN BOHEMIA 131

"Do you remember the day the Germans arrived in Plzen too?"
"Of course! In nineteen-thirty-nine I was a student and on March fourteen of that year the Slovaks declared their independence and the next day came the Munich announcement giving the Germans part of Bohemia. I remember how sad people were, especially my parents. It is not true, by the way, the Czech people were not ready to fight the Germans. From May to September of nineteen-thirty-eight many people reported to military barracks for training even before their draft notices arrived. Believe me we were ready to fight the Germans, but after Munich most people became too discouraged. The Germans forced me into labor at Skoda foundry, so I was luckier than many of my fellow students. In November of nineteen-thirty-nine there were student demonstrations in Prague and a medical student was shot, I think eight others were shot too. The Germans closed all the universities after that and sent students to concentration camps or forced labor camps under terrible conditions. So the students who stayed here were lucky. But I suppose what interests you is what I remember of the Americans. When we found out it was the Americans we all ran to the square and I found there were already many American tanks and jeeps there. I'll never forget the first American jeep I saw, it had the words *Beautiful Puppies* painted on its hood. That was about eight in the morning and there was a great many people already there celebrating. Then about ten in the morning there was snipping from the church tower and several other places. The *Wehrmach* had already left or surrendered but a few Gestapo troops had gotten together the night before and planned some resistance. We ran over to the church for a look and I lay flat against the side of the church until it was over. It didn't last long and they didn't put up much of a fight against the Americans. When I got back to our flat I saw parked outside our building a tank destroyer crew. They lived with us for several weeks, they were part of Patton's 3rd Army and not part of the 16th Armored Division. I still remember those men very clearly, each of them. There was a Lieutenant named Lamb

from Florida about 25, two men from New Jersey, Johnson and Stepanovich. There was a man named Bigley. I can't remember the name of the last man, but I can see his face clearly even now. You know I wanted to write Lt. Lamb for years but I lost his address and then just two weeks ago I found it inside a book after forty-five years!"

Mr. Flak took a drink of beer. "I remember a lot more Americans from that summer. Most of them wanted to meet Czech girls. Outside our building they had set up what you call a mess hall and I remember the first American meal I had was when the soldiers gave me hot dogs, I remember it clearly, even now."

Wilson watched Flak as he talked without interrupting him figuring that the more details he remembered the better the chances might be that something he didn't remember might surface. "I left for Prague that autumn to study and when I got back all the Americans were gone except for some soldiers in a motor pool in Slovany, but it was only a support group for some United Nations outfit."

"United Nations?"

"Yes, I'm sure of it. In forty-seven I got my notice for the Army and was sent to a post near the German border near Cheb and As. When the communists had their putsch in forty-eight most of us wanted to go to Prague and fight them, but we were confined to the barracks for ten days. Many people went over the German border then and we were supposed to stop them, I heard even a few army units defected because we were sent to stop one unit but by the time we got there they were gone! If you're wondering if I thought about defecting, I never considered it. I don't know why but I never thought about it."

"Not even when you were in prison? Wilson asked surprised.

"I was never in prison, that was my brother George."

"Your brother?"

"Yes, I've an older brother. I could introduce you to him, his story is much more interesting than mine. I was one of the lucky

A HOME IN BOHEMIA   133

ones."

Wilson took a deep breath and glanced at Havlicek. "Can you remember a soldier named Wilson, Harry Wilson?"

"No, I don't remember anyone named Wilson. I might have met him, of course, I met many soldiers that summer, but I remember only the names of the soldiers who lived in our house from the tank destroyer crew. Have you a photograph of this man?"

"No."

"Who was he?"

"My father."

"What did he look like?"

"Some people said he looked something like me."

Mr. Flak looked at Wilson more carefully. "It was a long time ago, you know, and there were a lot of soldiers here."

Suddenly, he doesn't remember so clearly, Wilson thought. Maybe he's making up a lot of it or just heard it from someone else.

"Would you like to meet my brother, he met a lot of Americans too?"

Wilson glanced at Havlicek, still unsure whether Havlicek had sent him on a goose chase. "Sure."

After Flak had left Wilson spoke softly, "Why did you send me on a goose chase Roman?"

"What do you mean, what's a goose chase?"

"It's when you send someone on a fool's errand?"

"You think I'm wasting your time?"

"I'm not sure."

"You learned something didn't you?"

"Sure the first jeep Flak saw had Beautiful Puppies written on its hood and his first American meal was hot dogs."

Havlicek smiled. "Don't get discouraged."

"Maybe he wasn't even in Plzen but in some village out in the boondocks."

"Boondocks?"
Wilson smiled. "In the sticks."
"You're talking in riddles."
"Welcome to Bohemia, brother."
"Well do you want to meet Mr. Flak's brother or do you want to give up?"
Wilson turned to look directly at his friend wondering once again if Havlicek had in someway manipulated him. "I've never given up on anything in my life except a marriage."
"I'd like to hear about your marriage someday."
"No you wouldn't."
"Why not?"
"Some things in life bring no one any honor, any knowledge or even any hope. They just exist as a swamp exists and you have to go around it or over it to get to someplace of meaning. But there's no profit to tell anyone about the first time you ended up in a swamp."
"I think there's something to learn even in a swamp."
"Maybe for a biologist like you who finds insects and bugs interesting."
"Life is life on every scale and you learn from little things as well as the big things. Sometimes in order to get to the big things you have to first learn little things."
Wilson studied Havlicek. Then smiled. "I guess when you need a guide to get around a swamp then you've got to trust the guide. So let's go find Flak."

"I was studying in France when the Germans invaded Czechoslovakia, then I taught in Egypt, then I joined the Czech Army in Palestine and fought at Tobruk," Flak said as Wilson and Havlicek listened. "I was in North Africa until June of nineteen-forty-three when I went to London and then fought on the continent. I returned to Czechoslovakia in June of nineteen-forty-five and was in the army until nineteen-forty-eight. I worked at Skoda as a French and

English translator until I was arrested in January of nineteen-fifty-two. My investigation lasted from January until September of nineteen-fifty-three. My trial lasted three days, then I was sentenced to death by the same judge who sentenced Dr. Horakova to death."

"Who was she?" Wilson asked.

For a moment Flak's face lost its inscrutability and betrayed surprise. "You don't know who she was?"

"No, I'm sorry I don't."

"I suppose it's normal that someone your age wouldn't know. She was a member of our Parliament and outspoken against the communists. They arrested her in June nineteen-fifty and had a show trial which lasted three days, like mine. They hung her there later at Pankrac prison in Prague. Our judge was Ludmila Brozova. She still lives in Plzen. They changed my sentence to imperpetuity."

"What did they charge you with?"

"Conspiracy and high treason."

"Conspiracy and treason?"

"Yes, I wrote letters to America to a soldier I had known in Germany. I was sent to Pankrac prison in Prague, then to Bory, then to Leopoldov prison, where I stayed until I was released in nineteen-sixty-four. My wife also was sent to prison."

"Why?"

Wilson thought he detected a trace of a smile at the corners of Flak's mouth. "She refused to denounce me. She was released after seven and a half years and was in Plzen when I got out."

"What did you do when they let you out?"

"I worked as a driver until I retired."

"How did you survive so long in prison?"

Jiri Flak became thoughtful and his focus shifted from Wilson to look out the window behind him. "I know of hundreds of people who committed suicide in the prisons because they couldn't take the beatings and other tortures any longer and I knew personally fifteen people who were beaten to death when I was at Bory prison. I can tell you I was a Christian before I was sent to prison and I still am a Christian."

"You've traveled and seen a lot before the war and now you've seen a lot here that most people never see in a life, what do you see in the future?"

Again Flak's expression became pensive and distant. "I don't know. It's not that I haven't thought about it, I've thought about it often. Once you've seen things in life that you never thought were possible, then all things become possible, the bad and the good. One side of me is pessimistic because we accepted evil too easily and that means we do not yet understand evil and have not questioned how we accepted it so easily for so long. Our young people need a new kind of education, different than the kind mine received. Their education must include moral persuasion."

"Why do you think so many Czech people were passive to tyranny after nineteen-forty-six?"

"Maybe because it came from our own people it was a case of self-denial. We had told ourselves for so many years that all our problems came from the Austrians, then we told ourselves it was the Germans. But when evil comes from your own people, some who are your neighbors you've grown up with, there is an element of self-denial because the evil is too close to yourself. Perhaps no one has the answer, perhaps it is in our blood."

For minutes after he had shaken Mr. Flak's hand Wilson sat quietly next to Havlicek in the pub. "He's a brave man," Wilson said at last.

"I know," Havlicek agreed, "but how do you know?"

"You can feel it in him, hear it in his voice, see it in his eyes."

"I thought you told me once you didn't believe in feelings?"

"I don't, they almost always lead you into swamps like a marriage with the wrong woman or to some other swamp."

"Sometimes you've got to trust your feelings."

"That's not very scientific and you're a scientist."

"Einstein once said, when the facts don't agree with your theory don't question your theory, but question the facts."

"I wonder why they didn't get rid of him, I thought the communists almost always got rid of their enemies through show trials?"

"They almost always did, but even the worst evil is imperfect."

"He seemed surprised maybe even insulted that I didn't know about this Dr. Horakova."

"She was the kind of symbol the communists couldn't stand because she was so honest and so virtuous and so fearless that her presence could inspire in other people the same qualities. So they hated her passionately, also she was a kind of mirror in which they saw their own reflections and by comparison they saw their own ugliness. They hated her more than anyone else. You should read about her."

"Maybe I will, but if she was what you say she was, then there must also be something heroic in Czech blood, which eliminates Flak's idea that the reason for the evil here lies in the blood."

"I don't think it's a question of what's in the blood but what's in the soul."

"So we're back to souls again?" Wilson said with a reluctant smile.

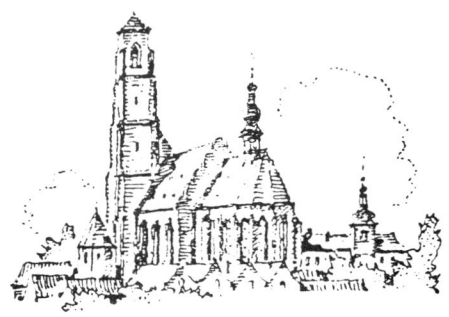

Chapter 25

Wilson found a small book on his desk. It was so thin and small that it could hardly be called a book. The front side had the words printed on it:

Dopisy Milady Horakova
Pankrac 24-27. 6. 1950

Wilson knew the Czech word for letter was *dopis*, so someone had left him a book of Dr. Horakova's letters from Pankrac Prison. He opened the little book with curiosity and found inside an envelope. He opened the envelope and found it stuffed with typewritten papers and a handwritten note clipped to the papers. The note was in broken English.

Dear Mr. Wilson:
I belong to an organization of former political prisoners, *Konfederance Politickych Veznu* - Plzen, and another member tell to me that you are looking to find an American soldier by name of Wilson, who you believe is father of you. I tell you to keep looking. I cannot say to you where to look, but it can be very close. I was in prison with a woman from Plzen and she had a child from an American soldier named Wilson. She tell to me so in prison.
I also give you gift of book Milada Horakova letters. She was great Czech woman. Our young people should know her life. I think you have interest in the suffering of Czech people under communists so I give you documents about history of Bory prison. You are teacher. Please say to students the truth about history.

- a friend

It must be a woman, Wilson reasoned, if she was in prison with another woman. But who knows what happened in those times, perhaps they threw people together like cattle. But she claimed to have known a woman from Plzen who knew an American soldier named Wilson and had a child by him. "I cannot say to you where to look but it can be very close." But there were two hundred thousand people living in Plzen. Not much help there.

Wilson leafed through the typewritten documents. They were double spaced and between the lines someone had handwritten in the English translation, though the handwriting was in places almost inscrutable. Wilson glanced at his class schedule which he had taped to the wall above his desk. He had an hour before his first afternoon class. He began to read one of the typed pages.

"Penitentiary Bory. Reminiscence and witness from the years about 1950. During the last days in March 1949, after my trial I was included in a prisoner's transport to Bory prison, at this time the State's Court prison number 1. There were 21 people in this group, mostly soldiers who had fought in the war and some from a former Czechoslovak Army. I welcome this transport to Bory after seven months of physical strain from staying in Secret Police and the State Court investigation. I left with the perspektive of 6 years hard confinement for alleged preparation of intrigues against the Republic and a betrayal of the Army. In my mind I hoped I could get some work outside and then maybe to escape from the work commando. I knew Plzen's environment very well and it was not so far to the border. I think many of us had this idea in the transport, but nobody speak of it. We were transported at this time handcuffed at the wrist to each other and guarded by about 20 policemen. In those days there were many transports, sometime to Plzen two transports a week. It was like a mill.

"In the State Court in Prague the prisoner's names were called to Pankrac Prison and they were lined up in groups and from this place they were taken to the State Court - the mill. Daily trials were in progress and sentences given for hundreds of years, including capital punishment too.

"Ruling communists got even with political antagonists, but at this time also with people who started to anticipate the dangers and would be enemies - it was probably the main reason for such big numbers of arrested people who took part in revolt in World War II against the Germans and from partisan's groups. These people were calculatedly eliminated and liquidated in trials controlled by Soviet consultants. The stay in Pankrac was reasonably acceptable in one way as the warder's manners were mostly fair. All these days atmosphere was pained with waiting and for some terrible thing, new arrested people kept coming with news from the outside. Some were optimistic. But at that time, February, myself I met Dr. Drtina on the corridor by chance - former Minister of Justice during the war known as Paval Svaty from BBC broadcasting for Czechoslovakia. He was deeply skeptical and didn't share our hopes to soon have better future. Soon after there was attempt to arrange his escape across the walls, shooting was heard and apparently there were some dead people - the attempt didn't turn out well. So the warders said.

"One day they brought a young man, very lively, to our cell on third B, he introduced himself as Petr Pujman and he was the real son of the writer Marie Pujmanova. Soon his mother visit him, which was exceptional, and she let him know that she pleaded for him with Antonin Zapotocky himself, but he only answered his nephew is there too and he can't do anything in it.

"But all of us remember with sorrow one day at Pankrac. That day the first executions were carried out, verdicts of the mill. Two young people, M. Choc and S. Sadek, were the victims. They waited for ratifying sentence on them and then, after ratifying of it they were taken from a prison wing to cells for people sentenced to death and they were executed in early morning hours. At this day there was a rumor going down in Pankrac the court couldn't muster a hangman.

"The very next day during the walk at 10 o'clock some detainees organized a pious ceremony. According to a special signal all of us stopped for a symbolic minute of silence for the killed people. Closely watching sergeant standing near to me came and asked me what does it mean. I explained to him and he stand aside and saluted. It was very strong experience for us that day, all of us had tears in our eyes on those two executed boy's memory.

"The trials was in progress at an incredible rate, the number of convicted persons increased and Pankrac was not able to hold them - new arrivals kept coming all the time and after an alleged attempt of a state take over. In February, 1949, all cells were crowded nearly to burst. At that time were about 4,000 soldiers in the garrison at castle Hradcany - at least the soldiers brought to Pankrac insisted on it. Walking yards were packed by uniforms and at the same time the prison routine tightened up. We heard stories that a part of army should occupy radio, central offices and set prisoners free from Pankrac and Bory with help of tanks and motorized corps. But it did not come true.

"For this reason it was necessary to send convicted people to prisons and camps without regard to their appeal or legal proceedings. Myself I never got the written verdict, like thousands of others.

"We came to Plzen central train station about 10 o'clock in a line of 21 people in chains going to exit under strong escort. People looked at us in wonder, amazement, but also fear.

"We were taken in trucks with canvas tops to the Bory Prison main corridor. There we quickly realized things at Bory were much different than at Pankrac. There was terrible shouting and swearing. There were *'bachar'* - goons running about with clubs and rubber truncheons hitting people. One goon in particular I remember because he was small and had the face of a rat and had decorations from 8th British Army that many Czech men fought with in Africa. At first I thought I landed in another world, inhuman world. We had our heads shaved and stripped naked standing in rows in the yard. There we were given a warning of what happened to us if we did not obey. A prisoner was brought from a cell with chains on legs. To walk he had to lift chains with a rope. He was unshaven and dirty. We met for a moment his eyes. So much hopelessness. He had attempted to escape.

"Then the warder stepped forward. He was a handsome young man with happy look on his face, Vaclev Brabec.

"The prisoner in chains had collapsed and Brabec kicked him several times to revive him. It did not work so they threw water on him. That didn't work so they drug him away into the cells and soon we could hear screams and blows on flesh.

"Brabec came back looking pleased. We look at him with terror never having heard something so inhuman.

"We quickly learned what it meant when they said those who survive the punishment cells were favored by God. The most horrible period since the beginning of Bory prison came the came at the beginning of the 50's. At that time General Heliodor Pika was executed. He was sentenced by the Government Military Tribunal for alleged high treason to death. He was the former military attache of our London cabinet in Moscow during the war. Before he was executed he had smoked his last cigarette. A supervisor, Sgt. Petelik, one of the good and decent supervisors, father of two small children, picked up that cigarette butt after the execution. And Sgt. Petelik payed for it with his life.

"He arranged with one prisoner, Stanislav Broj, a former parlimentarian for Rokycany, that he would give the end of the cigarette to General Pika's wife. Nobody is sure about how this all came to light, even Broj, and former Major Rene Cerny were executed. Six supervisors and other prisoners were also sentenced to years of punishment. The case of the alleged conspiracy in a prison was staged and prepared by Lieutenant Strojin. The examiner of the case was Cely Satarsik. The proceedings took place in of all places the Plzner theater! At the end of the proceedings the carefully seated audience shouted, "Hang them! Hang them!"

Wilson stood and went to the end of his office where curtains partitioned off an area for storage of school supplies and teachers kept bottles of refreshment on a shelf. He picked up his bottle of wine and took a drink. They murdered three men because of a cigarette butt, Wilson thought. But not before they beat them to a pulp. It seemed a kind of grotesque fantasy, except that it had happened right in Plzen. Maybe there were even ghosts still hovering among the rotted bricks. He took another drink of wine and returned to his desk.

"In 1968 there was a kind of inquiry into this horrible show trial in the Plzen theater. One man testified that before the executions when he was standing guard with another guard they heard the rattling of chains in a cell and pushed open the peep hole for a look. They saw something difficult to identify as human. Even at a close look you couldn't identify who he was because of the blood and swelling from his neck up. Then Capt. Safarik said, 'Well, this is one of them who was a guard, don't you recognize him? This is This is Sergeant Petelik!'

"Engineer Jan Tykvart gave testimony about the last hours of these three men condemned to death, he was a one-time prisoner and watchman of the corridor in Pankrac prison. 'I went down there and Petelik was in one of the cells as was Deputy Broj and Major Cerny, who was lying in bed the last two days. Because the other guards were relaxing outside on a bench I had a chance to stay a little longer than normal with Broj, who I knew in former times. I asked him if there was anything I could get him and he answered that he needed a stronger pair of glasses so he could write his final message to his children. So I got him some and put in a stronger light bulb in his cell. I asked him how he had come into such a terrible end? And he answered he didn't know anything about it, that they even made him memorize his lines for his trial. He said all had to learn their parts by heart beforehand....'"

Wilson bolted up toppling his chair onto the floor and jerked the curtains open and drank from his bottle. When he returned to his desk he found the final page of the report and skipped to the last paragraph.

"Scores of years have passed, yet Bory Prison is still towering over the Litice River Dam as a memorial to the Czechoslovak *gulag,* where the shouts of pain and desperation still echo from its sick walls. The souls and hearts of those who remember have been permanently scared by the afflicted sufferings and memories of the unhappy people who found their hell on earth there. And you, dear reader, who had the patience to read these testimonies, if you happen to pass by Bory prison on a walk with your family, stop for a moment and give a brief moment of honor to those who suffered and died for you and your future. And before I close, I can't leave one question unasked, a question I feel I have a full right to ask, friends, you didn't know about all this? None of you? About anything?'"

Wilson stood up, he was dimly aware that the bell had rung to signal the beginning of his next class. He entered his classroom from the door at the read which connected his office. His class stood in unison but Wilson stared straight ahead with a frown and told them to sit down. He took roll and gave a reading assignment so he would not have to lecture. As his class read, Wilson moved to stand by a window and stared out at the grey sky over the rooftops of Plzen. The last words of the political prisoner kept returning to him, "Friends, you didn't know about all this? None of you? About anything?"

Wilson had known, of course. He had known about *gulags* like Bory and the details he didn't know he avoided knowing.

Chapter 26

Some Czechs didn't fail to resist, Wilson thought, as he stood in the cold and falling sleet across the street from Bory prison at the southern edge of Plzen. Some men and women didn't fail to resist and the bastards put them in prison or killed them. Like Milada Horakova. When he saw her photograph Wilson felt a shock. Her face was what he remembered the face of his kindergarten teacher, Mrs. Kimble, looked like.

There are some faces from boyhood, he thought, that stay with a man almost as long as the faces of his mother and father do because they generate a sense of love and trust. Like the memory of Mrs. Kimble.

Looking at the main gate of Bory prison, Wilson felt anger. How could anyone harm a face with such integrity and kindness as the face of Dr. Horakova? Maybe it was a face of such obvious integrity, intelligence and kindness that it made her an obvious enemy of the communists? Maybe they saw her as a symbol too dangerous to be allowed to survive? But why didn't the good men in this country take up arms and revolt and tear down places like Bory prison brick by brick? Thousands of Czech men fought in foreign armies against the Germans, so they knew how to fight. When they saw their own people being thrown into prison and tortured, why didn't they revolt and take up arms like the Greeks did against the Greek communists? Was it possible there really was a difference in blood? Damn the communists, but they were just common thugs and criminals. And damn the men who were too afraid to defend what was good and decent and for being too afraid to protect their own people from the thugs and criminals.

If something so basic as courage could be taught or eliminated then wasn't it possible you could have behaved the same if you had been born in Plzen?

Wilson's eyes narrowed as he studied the main gate of the prison and the policeman who stood guard. The bastards. All of them. Damn the Americans too who stopped Patton from going on to liberate Prague before the communists got there. Damn them and let their souls rot in some place as miserable as Bory prison.

Souls! How was it that the world seemed to have refined methods of promoting those with the most timid souls to the positions of defending civilization against barbarians? They promote them through graduate schools in universities where they write timid dissertations calculated never to offend anyone. Then a select few are hired for positions in the government, like the State Department, where once again they answer questions with answers calculated never to contradict what is "politically correct." Then they work over desks for years to climb up the ladder and one fine day they are sitting and smiling across from a Hitler, a Stalin, a Malinkov or a Sadem Husein. And guess who always wins the so-called negotiations? Is it any wonder the thugs always win when we have a system guaranteed to promote the timid and punish the strong? If we used the same system to select an Olympic team we'd finish somewhere above Uruguay and behind Argentina.

Her name was Ludmila Brozova, Wilson learned. She was said to be the judge who sentenced Milada Horakova to be hung. They said she still lived in Plzen, retired on pension. He should kill her, he thought, if he ever met her. He should grab her and break her neck with a hammer lock, like he'd seen wrestlers do on television. And he should whisper into her ear the name of Horakova so she would understand justice before he broke her neck.

It would be the only meaningful thing he ever did in his life.

Standing in the cold as the sleet collected on his shoulders and cap and formed a thin crust, he reflected he had spent his life indulging in meaningless things like sports and at the same time accepted the milky dogma that it was developing his character. But he had never once in his life had to defend anything good against evil. Now a barbarian was living comfortably only a few minutes away who had helped murder one of the most civilized women in Europe or the world.

Wilson turned and began walking disconsolately back toward the city center. He wouldn't kill her, he realized. She was an old woman. Her kind were hardly worth killing when they were young. Maybe they deserved to be killed, but they were not worth killing. A man dirtied his hands having anything to do with them. You kill a skunk and it still smells up everything it touches. He felt defeated having come face-to-face with the truth he had never once in his life defended something from barbarians despite the fact he had lived during a period of history when the worst barbarians had controlled half of Europe. A more depressing thought was that he didn't know whether he would have fought them if he had been born in Bohemia.

The sleet had turned to soft falling snowflakes and Wilson felt a storm of discontent as he wondered if he would have been like those who simply fled over the border to save their own rear ends. Damn, how could you be sure what you would have done? Everything in this country was Kafka-like. Nothing was clear. He felt a sense of weariness. The idea that he would have run away defeated him.

As he shuffled along through the snow his thoughts landed on his basketball team. His team continued to violate all that he loved about basketball and sports. The idea of pretending not to notice their lack of heart couldn't be reconciled.

After every game he fought back the impulse to walk away from it and quit. He couldn't stand any longer, he thought, watching his players loaf through another loss and take losing so calmly. But it seemed just as repulsive to quit before the season ended.

Sometimes, he anguished, a man found himself trapped in a position where he violated one principle in order not to violate another principle. It was a no win position in which no matter what he did, he would feel like a loser.

That seemed to be the meaning of life in Bohemia. Damn Kafka.

As he had over the past few weeks, he tried to remember what it was in Turgenev's book, *First Love,* that he had talked about with Zoya. But the words wouldn't come to him.

Chapter 27

"You were wrong about the war," Havlicek remarked.

"There's nothing like being completely wrong. But right up until the day before they started bombing Baghdad I thought they would make a deal. I hope the hell they know what they're doing and all their high tech toys work and they can get it over quickly."

"Do you think it will be over quickly?"

Wilson smiled in contemplation. "Why ask a man who picked the losing horse? Maybe this is a preview of the twenty-first century war, laser guided smart bombs, infra red spy cameras in space to make war at night as easy as war in the daylight. Maybe they will no longer need grunts on the ground getting their asses shot at."

"What are grunts?"

"Soldiers who carry rifles, eat cold food, sleep in the mud and get their asses shot at by other soldiers."

"Were you ever a grunt?"

"No."

"What did your father do in the army?"

"I don't know."

"Have you found anyone yet who knew him in Plzen?"

"Nope."

"Are you still looking?"

Wilson looked out the window of Havlicek's office. It was a grey January afternoon with some dusting snow falling and being blown by a tail wind on the sidewalks in the same way wind pushes small clouds of dust in the desert. "Have you got anymore of that Irish coffee?"

"You mean coffee with rum?"

Wilson nodded.

"Coming up, but you didn't answer my question, are you still looking for someone who knew your father?"

"Sort of."

"Well either you are or you aren't?"

"I've put it on hold."

"That means you've stopped?"

"No, that means I'm taking a break."

"But you told me that you would keep looking until you found someone who knew him."

Wilson smiled at his reflection in the window pane and turned toward Havlicek. "I know what I said, but have you ever started a search for one thing and ended up learning something that made the original objective seem unimportant compared to the thing you learned by accident?"

"Sure, it happens all the time in science. What have you learned?"

"Nothing I didn't already know before I started, such as political prisoners, brutality, suffering, betrayals, lies and selfishness. But when you see it up close in a human face and with a name then it becomes personal in a way that penetrates into you so that you can't walk away from it because it follows you. After a time it feels like an open wound that won't heal and you have to take a break."

"Tell me about some of the faces and names you discovered in your search."

"The face of Milada Horakova."

Havlicek stood and poured two cups of boiling water into coffee grounds and then laced each cup with some rum. "It was a kind of lynching like in the old West and so ugly that it became the symbol for all the ugliness that happened here under the communists. Did you mean her face was one you couldn't walk away from?"

Wilson nodded. "It had such intelligence and humanity in it, that

I couldn't imagine anyone would want to harm her, but only a monster. Then I went out to have a look at Bory prison."

"You didn't know about Bory?"

"No."

"How much do you know now about what happened there?"

"About as much as I can stand."

"How much can you stand?"

"Not much. It seems to make me feel a little crazy."

"You mean such things as the idea of living here among people who you know were informers or prison guards who tortured prisoners? Such as knowing that you see them everyday in the streetcars and shops. Such as knowing you probably eat with them in canteens and drink with them in pubs. Such as knowing that you probably even work with a few, so you never really know which face is your friend or your natural enemy, so you begin to see something evil in faces instead of seeing something good. In time a poison works its way into your system. Can you still say to me you are happy to be here among us?"

"Us?"

"Sure. How do you know I wasn't an informer or collaborator?"

Wilson studied his colleague. "I know."

"No, you don't. When you've lived here you learn you can't trust anyone. So you can never say 'I know.' Not here. Maybe someday."

"I thought you were the one who believed in good and bad souls?"

Havlicek smiled. "Do you think you can feel my soul?"

"Don't get carried away, I never said that."

"You implied it."

"I only meant that I felt I could trust you."

"Trust me or trust what is inside me?"

"Okay, have it your way."

"Is the idea of living here now dark and gloomy?"

"When I heard that the judge who sentenced Milada Horakova

to be hung was still alive and living here in Plzen, all I could think about was getting my hands on her neck. I never knew that kind of thing existed in me before. Oh, I've met some people I disliked enough I felt like socking them in the jaw, but I never wanted to kill another person."

"It's like I said, when you live here long enough being exposed to poison, in the end, it infects you too and you have to fight against the thinking it can grow."

Wilson turned to look back out the window and his voice became as wintry as the weather. "After seeing Bory prison I thought maybe what has gone wrong with modern man is he's forgotten how to be really angry at barbarians because he has been put to sleep by words and intellectual rituals that make people feel good, as if they're actually resisting evil, when in fact they've done nothing. I tried to think of how a man could resist evil without becoming as bad as the evil he's against. Have you ever read the novel, *Zorba The Greek?*"

"Yes, it's one of my favorite books."

"Do you remember the scene where the mob in the village has gathered outside the church because the beautiful widow is inside who they want to kill?"

"Of course, who could forget it."

"Then you remember even the women of the village stood in the back of the crowd and screamed for the widow's death. And what was her sin, her sin was being born with beauty and so they murdered her out of envy and jealousy, not for some broken law they claimed. And only one man came to her defense, an uneducated man. Zorba. That's the kind of man I'd like to be. To be decent and brave and primitive enough that I could do what is right instinctively. So I wouldn't be satisfied with words and intellectual rituals and think I've done something when I've done nothing. I think Zorba would go out to Slovany and find that judge and break her neck - but I can't. I'm bogged down in intellectual arguments and they paralyze me. I've been exposed to the modern disease of words and been seduced by them. Another thought came to me returning from Bory prison. Perhaps my father might have actually done something I've never managed to do."

"What?"

"Perhaps he actually defended civilization against barbarians with his own sweat and guts. That would mean he was one rung above me on the humanity ladder."

"Life is full of surprises!"

"But one thing I still don't understand after all the people I've talked to, is how so many people could have gone along with the communists for so long."

"What do you mean, gone along with?"

"I mean all the men I talked to who were old enough to have known my father all told me they had good educations and they went to school before the communists took over. Even now they think they had a good education, yet that system produced a population that allowed the communists to come to power. I can understand how many people might have felt bitterness toward the West for abandoning them to Hitler, but it can't be used as an excuse to jump into bed with communists."

"I think you're right about one thing, anytime a culture turns away from what is human for something inhuman, it reveals a failure in its education system. The difference should be taught in schools. But what happened here is more complicated than you understand. Before the war sympathy for communism in intellectual circles was common across all Western Europe. The communists were clever in borrowing socialist ideas and appearing to be something with roots in the lives of everyday working people. And when you speak of education, what is it that you really mean? A nation's education must include its literature. Consider the literature you must have read growing up. How many stories did you read of pioneers and cowboys before you entered school? Each time you read one of those folk tales some-

A HOME IN BOHEMIA   155

thing took root in you as surely as something took root in the Greek boy who read Homer: the idea of something heroic."

Havlicek took a drink of his coffee and continued. "Literature expresses a nation's attitude toward life, but consider that we were a free nation only from nineteen-eighteen until nineteen-thirty-eight. We didn't have the time to develop through literature a national identity and attitude toward life that was heroic. And despite the freedom America has had since the end of World War II, where are your replacements for such writers as Faulkner, Steinbeck and Hemingway? You had two hundred years of independence to develop your national literature and then in less than one generation you declined into mediocrity. But no one, such as the Germans or Russians forced you to decline. So what do you expect of a small country who had only twenty years of freedom in the whole twentieth century? It's easy for someone to judge our education and culture as a failure because we didn't resist the Germans with arms or because we degenerated under communism by destroying our best people, such as Horakova, but it's not as simple as you imagine it to be. The real history is more complicated."

Wilson studied his coffee and heaved. His shoulders rose and fell. "You make it sound rather hopeless, as if we're all in a ship that is taking on water at sea and there are no lifeboats or rescue ships on the horizon."

"No it's not hopeless. To feel hopeless is to dismiss the human spirit. Look at yourself."

Wilson smiled and lifted his eyebrows. "I'd rather not."

"You came to our school and our students are better for it. I've seen the change in some of them, I've heard some of them talking about the ideas you've given them. You think you're not accomplishing anything or very little, but that isn't true. It's just that we won't see any results of it for years. But that's the nature of good education. It is planting ideas that take root and then, like a fruit tree, the fruit comes years later. You didn't think you could produce a championship basketball team in one year did you?

"I don't think I could produce one here in my lifetime."

"Oh, you don't believe that nonsense. I know they've disappointed you, I've come to see them play, but those boys have never been exposed to good fundamentals and they have not been exposed to the level of competition you knew as a boy. So how do you expect them to grasp what a championship is? It seems to me it's a question again of education - being exposed to something. A good education really consists of a hundred different things you receive outside of a school room. Wasn't it Mark Twain who remarked, 'Never let school get in the way of your education!'"

Wilson smiled. "Where in the hell did you learn that?"

"Never mind, but isn't it true? So don't give me any nonsense about you can't build a championship team here. But it will require patience and time, just as a good culture can be built here, even after fifty years of occupation, because I believe in the human spirit and its ability to overcome false religions and political empires. So when are you going to get back to the business of looking for someone who remembers your father?" Havlicek finished with his mischievous grin.

"Soon."

"How soon?"

"Give me a break, will you?"

"Why should I, do you give your basketball players a break when they are loafing?"

"You sound like a coach."

"I've done some coaching before. You want some names of old communists to talk to, you might find them interesting?"

"I doubt they'd want to talk to me."

"You'd be surprised. Some people really believed in it and would be only too happy to talk to you."

"Sure give me their names. By the way have you ever read a novel by Ivan Turgenev called *First Love?*"

"Why?"
"I need a copy, in English if possible."
"I'll ask around. I've seen copies of it, but it might be out of print."

Chapter 28

Wilson stood in the snow outside the Electra theater on Moskevska street waiting for Martina Bellekova. When he had invited her to a film she chose *"Silkwoodova."* Wilson knew it was about an American woman by the name of Karen Silkwood, who worked in a nuclear laboratory in Oklahoma. Newspapers wrote she had collected information about safety violations at her laboratory concerning radiation to give to a reporter for the *New York Times*. On the night of the meeting with the reporter she was killed in an auto accident. Some people thought it wasn't an accident but a murder.

Wilson wasn't interested in seeing *Silkwoodova*, but decided not to make an issue over it. Waiting in the cold he thought about Martina. Often he felt awkward and somewhat self-conscious around her because of their strained communications. He wondered if she could be as innocent as she seemed at times. It seemed unlikely. She had studied at a university in Prague and students there must be like students everywhere. They drank beer and flirted and dated just like students in American universities. And she must have had relationships with Czech men after school, so she couldn't be as innocent as she appeared.

Wilson sat stiffly through the movie. He liked it even less than he imagined he would. He was relieved when at last the film ended and they trailed out of the theater, along with the rest of the small crowd, back into the cold and snow packed sidewalks. "Where to?" Wilson asked.

"I don't care, how about the *vinarna* our English class sometimes goes to?"

"I've never liked that place, how about the gril across the street?" She nodded agreement.

"Did you enjoy the film?" Wilson asked after they had taken their first drink of beer.

"That's not the right word. I'm happy to have seen it but I don't feel happy to know that it's a true story. It reminds me too much of what went on in this country for so long."

"How do you mean?"

"For example, the man in the lab who was doctoring the x-rays of the fuel rods, his first concern was the security of his comfortable job and the health of his friends and other workers was less important to him. Somehow he was able to block out his moral responsibility to other people. That is what spread from the top of our culture to the bottom under the communists. No one knows how long it will take to change this kind of thinking once it has worked its way into the psychology of people."

"What do you think, can it be changed here?" Wilson watched her smile and run a finger through strands of her hair, as she often did when she was in class. "I suppose we are questioning something that deals with the spiritual condition of people in general everywhere, not just here."

"Okay. What do you think?"

"That's almost a kind of religious question."

"Yes, I suppose so. You want to skip it?"

"No, I'm just thinking about it," she answered.

Her voice became softer so he had to lean toward her slightly. "I think man in general is bad by nature but I think certain men and women are born with a good nature so that there is always hope for change in society."

"By nature, you mean the soul of men?"

She smiled again and for a moment their eyes locked. "I'm not sure I believe in such a thing as a soul."

"Then you don't believe in God?"
"No."
"Have you ever gone to church?"
"Yes, but not for the purpose of religion."
"What?"
"I went to a midnight Christmas service to hear the music."
Wilson nodded and smiled.
"And do you believe in God?" she asked.
"Sometimes."
"I think either you do or you don't," Martina Bellekova said with a polite smile.
"I guess the jury is still out for me."
"What does that mean?"
"It means I'm not smart enough to figure it out."
"You make it sound like some kind of mystery, like a detective novel."
"Well, I think it is a mystery and maybe you have to be a kind of detective to figure it out and get to some truth."
"I've more faith in logic and reason in solving problems."
"Some things aren't logical and if you depend on reason you only frustrate yourself. I don't think you can compare economics to things like religion."
"But there are principles that take superstition and mystery out of things."
Wilson nodded.
"Well, what's your opinion of the nature of man?"
"Do you mean whether he was born with a bad or good nature?"
"Yes."
"I think I'll have a glass of wine, would you like to switch too?"
"Yes."
"Red or white?"
"It doesn't matter."
Wilson ordered some *tokajsky*.
"Well what's your opinion?"

A HOME IN BOHEMIA 161

"You know, Havlicek believes in souls and I sort of play the devil's advocate when - "

"What's a devil's advocate?"

"It's when you take a position that you do not necessarily agree with in order to promote a healthy argument. So with Roman I take a position that there is no such thing as a soul. He counters with the fact that there is scientific evidence now that certain particles can traverse space without seeming to move. It contradicts all we previously understood about physics. Sometimes all we can say about something is that we don't know. Roman believes, for example, that some souls are more dense than others which explains why we feel as we do about certain people, we feel their density or lack of it, is what Roman seems to be saying. He thinks I have a dense soul."

"You seem to be avoiding my question, what's your opinion."

"It sounded ridiculous."

"You don't believe you have a soul?"

"I didn't say that," Wilson said taking a drink of *tokajsky* and enjoying the vermouth-like taste.

"Can't you just say what it is you believe?"

"I guess the jury is out."

"I think you're just avoiding my question."

"No, I'm not. I just can't figure it out."

"In the film tonight, they mentioned Hanford. Is that the same Hanford where you're from?"

"The same one."

"Do you think they have the same problems at Hanford as they showed in the film?"

Wilson nodded. "Bigger because Hanford is ten times as big as the laboratory shown in the film. There's been a lot of people killed at Hanford over the years."

"Have you known anyone who has been killed?"

"Yeah, I have."

"Anyone close to you?"

"Yes, very close."
"Can you talk about it?"
"Sure."
"Who did you know who was killed?"
"My brother."
Their eyes locked for a moment. "You're not making a joke?"
"No joke. He's been dead for about ten years."
"How did he die."
"Like most of them, he got cancer. Phil got cancer of the thyroid and before they diagnosed it, it spread."
"Couldn't it have been from something else beside radiation?"
"Maybe. But when you study the people who lived there then a kind of pattern becomes obvious. Thyroid problems from the leaked radio active iodine one-thirty-one. Thyroid problems became epidemic. The radiation got into everything, the water, milk, fish, the air. One government study revealed that children who were there when Phil and I grew up were exposed to a total radioactivity equal to thirty-four thousand x-rays! No one got that much, of course, but we got exposed to more than enough to cause about any cancer you can imagine."
"Was he older or younger than you?"
"He was younger."
"So in theory then you've been exposed to more than he was?"
Wilson smiled. "In theory I should be dead. Like I said, logic and reason can't explain everything."
"How do you explain the fact you're alive - when some others died from it?"
"Maybe an act of God."
"Are you playing the devil's advocate now?"
"Maybe."
"Be serious, what's your opinion."
Wilson ordered another round of *tokajsky*. "I can't explain it. I don't think anybody can. We know cigarettes cause lung cancer, but not everybody gets lung cancer from smoking cigarettes.

Nobody ever said life's fair."

"But we know that smoking and lung cancer has something to do with genetics. You and your brother had the same genes. You sound a little bitter."

"Like I told Havlicek, I'm not a scientist or philosopher. But as a matter of fact my brother had more to live for than me and it would have been better for me to die than him."

"How do you mean?"

"He had a wife and two children. A good job."

"He was different than you?"

"Most people say he was much different. Had a better personality they say."

"How?"

"Well people say I'm difficult to get along with or haven't you noticed?"

Martina Bellekova glanced at him without answering. "What kind of things did you love as a boy?"

"Same things I love now. Nature. The desert, Hanford is in the desert. When you grow up in the desert then no matter where you go or live after that there is always a hunger to get back to where it is calm and quiet, like the desert. But it's different today because a lot of people have moved there from the city. They bring motor homes and recreational vehicles and it destroys the calm and quiet. Now people who grew up there have only a memory. But even the memory has a kind of magnetism that makes you want to go back."

"Like the memory of your brother?"

Wilson frowned. "I guess the good things in life have a way of becoming part of you. What things do you love in life?"

She combed the ends of her hair with finger tips, finally she spoke in a low voice, "I think I'm like you, I love nature."

Wilson waited for her to continue or to enlarge on what she loved in nature. But after a few seconds he realized that was all she was going to say. He felt a blade of irritation cut at him; she was throwing up a wall again.

"I suppose we'd better get going, unless you'd like another glass of wine?" Wilson said trying to hide his irritation.

"No thanks, I've had enough."

Wilson caught the waiter's eye and paid their tab and they shouldered into their jackets and went back outside to the snow and cold. It had snowed enough that the fresh snow had covered the hardened patches on the sidewalk and the only sound was the crunch of snow under foot as they walked. Wilson hesitated and then said good night politely to her at the front entrance of her apartment building and turned quickly to hike to his streetcar.

At home he opened his refrigerator for a beer and decided beer wasn't what he wanted. He considered wine. That wasn't what he wanted either and slammed the refrigerator door shut. What he wanted, he reasoned, standing by his kitchen window looking out into the darkness and lights of Plzen, was to have some real communications with Martina Bellekova. He wanted some honest exchanges that left something soothing afterward instead of the rawness that sparring with words left.

After an evening with Martina Bellekova there was always a feeling of exile in a land full of crosscurrents and mirages that hinted of something satisfying and good just over the horizon. It was in her eyes the way she often glanced at him, in the way her voice lowered and softened sometimes when they were alone. The idea of something fulfilling kept Wilson trying to penetrate behind the walls she threw up.

Wilson opened his refrigerator door again, as if he might find something in it that he had overlooked, then slammed it shut again.

Chapter 29

After his last class Wilson collected some odds and ends off his desk top and jammed them into his briefcase. He opened a drawer and picked up the little book on Dr. Milada Horakova and stood motionless for long moments looking at it with a frown before he shoved it into his briefcase. Her name churned up the same feeling in his stomach that he felt when he had read about the political prisoners guillotined in Dresden or when he had read about the political prisoners at Bory prison.

Outside the school it was snowing lightly, but in the evening dusk it made a pleasant feel against the skin after being indoors all day. Instead of boarding his streetcar at his usual stop he crossed the street and entered the gril.

He found a table in a corner that was empty and felt some fatigue once he was out of his overcoat and off his feet.

"*Pivo,*" Wilson said to the familiar waiter. After his first drink of beer he sighed and pulled out the little book from his briefcase that someone had left on his desk the week before. He had avoided looking at the book during the week. On the fly page inside the front cover was a portrait of Dr. Horakova, once again Wilson admired her thoughtful expression and intelligence eyes. As he thumbed through the opening text he felt some relief to find it was all in Czech language. But when he came to the first photo copy of her first letter from prison, he noticed someone had written in an English translation.

"Damn," Wilson muttered, it all happened a long time ago. I can't do anything about it now. No one can do anything about it now. So I should close the book and forget it. I know damn well

I'll feel lousy after reading it. So do yourself a favor and close the book.

Wilson closed the book and with his finger tips gently pushed it away from himself toward the center of the table. Well done, coward. Like the political prisoner wrote in his story, "Friends, I feel I have the right to ask, you didn't know about this? Any of this?"

You didn't want to know about it in America and you don't want to know about it now. What is it are you afraid of? What have you been running away from all these years? When you sat in front of the television last winter watching the revolution and staring at the faces in the streets, what was it that you were looking for? Why did you feel such discontent after watching the revolution?

All right, I'll read it. It won't change anything. Nothing good can come of it. Whoever left it on my desk was just wasting their time. Wilson reached for the book and opened it to the page with the first letter.

          24 June, 1950
          Pankrac prison

My Dearly Beloved:
"I read somewhere not long ago the letter is just like a light and a star's rays. It comes to people and radiates to them often, even when it's source burst out and doesn't exist for a long time. And still it makes people clear and illuminates to them. It will be the same with this, my letter. It will soothe and kiss you by my words even at this time, when already the hand writing will be distant from you. "Don't cry for me too much," says Kozik in one of his poems we used to read in the hospital at Terezin.* Please, read this poem together with this letter and do according to those words. Really don't cry and don't torture your hearts with sadness. Sometimes it's very difficult to stand without tears when the Lord

sends down his test and misery...."

Wilson finished his beer and thought how good a taste of bourbon would be at that moment. Wilson ordered a whiskey.
He began the second letter which was undated but carried an official's stamp, number 1326. The third letter was dated, Sunday, June 25, 1950, 7 a.m. It was to her sister. The fourth was written to her mother-in-law, also on June 25. Then a fifth letter on June 25 to relatives. Wilson skimmed the letters.

In his mind he calculated how many hours she had to live. The thought tightened his stomach. He tasted his whiskey. Why didn't somebody do something? He ordered another whiskey.

The next letter was written on Monday, June 26 at eight in the morning. It was to another relative. She's got less than twenty-four hours to live, Wilson thought. Where was President Truman? Where was the United Nations? I guess they were up to their asses with Korea. And where were the bastards who thought it was such a good idea to stop Patton in Plzen?

The next letter was undated. It was addressed to, "My only little daughter Jane." Wilson read it.

The next letter was written to "My Dear Boy, Dearest Man," on Monday at 1 p.m. She's got sixteen hours to go, Wilson thought.

"Until the 27th of September it was, for nearly 26 years we loved each other, the first line of your poem. Then it turned over tragically and suddenly. I'm writing to you like I write the others and even I don't know if you are alive or if it's possible for you to read these words. This is the biggest pain of my heart that I don't know anything about you and I have not even the saddest sureness, and maybe I live my last hours of my life...Maybe it will be explained to me somewhere, where our souls will meet again..."

Wilson chewed his lip. The bastards. He turned the pages to the final letter. It was dated June 27, 2:30 a.m. Two and a half hours to go, Wilson thought.

My Dearest:

"Still several words....I feel entirely calm and I'm ready. The priest was by me, and even if Dr. Kucera couldn't come, it was a great reassurance to me ...Go to the meadows and forests, there you'll find a part of me in the smell of flowers, go to the fields, look at the beauty and we'll be together everywhere. Look at the people surrounding you and I'll reflect in everybody's face by something. I'm not embarrassed and desperate - I don't pretend, everything is so calm in me....I'm modest and resigned to God's fate - he determined me this test and I'm going through it with only this wish: to fulfill God's laws and to keep my honest name...This way I can fly to fields and meadows, hillsides and lakes, to the mountains and also the lowlands...The birds are waking up - the sun is rising. I go with my head up - it's necessary to know how to lose too. It's not a shame. With love, only and only yours."

Milada

Wilson closed the book. It was over, he thought. Her time ran out. They liquidated her. The cowards didn't even have the honor to give her letters to her family. For forty years the cowards hid her letters.
And for the last forty years what have you been doing, Wilson thought? You've been playing games. You grew up to be David Wilson, a modern man. But when all the smoke clears you're no better than the timid bastards who stopped Patton.
Well now you have a chance to do something - after forty years. You know where she lives. You know what Zorba would have done and didn't you tell Havlicek that you'd like to be a man like Zorba? Well nothing is stopping you - except you.
Wilson paid for his drinks and lifted his jacket from the wooden peg. He saw a couple of teachers from his school and he nodded

at them without smiling. He caught a streetcar at his stop but instead of going home he got off on Moskevska and rode a trolleybus to Slovany and then another streetcar. He began walking until he found the number and went to the front entrance to check the registry. There it was, Ludmila Brozova. He stood looking at it, but didn't press the buzzer. He turned and walked across the street and stood against a building staring up at the rows of yellow lights in the dark.

He could break her neck easily, he thought. Or he could choke her as some of the prisoners must have died whose necks didn't break on impact. He could do it either way. It started to snow again and Wilson continued looking up at the rows of yellow windows across the street in the apartment building.

Instead of going home he found himself back at his office. He found Roman Havlicek sitting in his chair at his desk.

"I heard someone saw you at the gril and they said you looked sad and gloomy, so I thought I'd come and cheer you up."

"You're sitting in my chair."

"I know."

"I'd appreciate it if you'd move your ass out of my chair and my office, I'd like to be alone."

"They were right, you're sad and gloomy."

"Dammit, Havlicek, knock off the crap and clear out."

"You look grim enough to strangle someone," Havlicek said with a smile, as he stood up to leave.

Wilson's voice was hoarse. "Some people deserve to be strangled and I wish to God I was the man for it."

Havlicek hesitated and leaned against the wall. "How about a drink?"

Wilson slumped in his chair. "Fine, but just shut up, okay."

Havlicek smiled and opened his briefcase he had brought along and pulled out a bottle and two glasses. He poured two glasses of whisky and pushed one across the desk toward Wilson. "Dr. Havlicek's special remedy, I'm told you like bourbon."

"Shut up dammit," Wilson said taking the glass and draining it in a gulp.

"Do you feel like talking about it?"

"No, not with you," Wilson answered taking the new drink Havlicek poured.

"What's the matter with me?"

"You're a Czech."

"But I've always been a Czech and you always knew I was a Czech."

"But I didn't always know what a Czech was."

"And you know now?"

Wilson slowly lifted his head to look at Roman Havlicek. "Yeah, I know now. They are no good son of a bitches who won't fight for anything."

Havlicek smiled slowly. "Tell me more about it."

"I don't want to tell you or any other Czech about it. I want you to get your ass out of my office."

"I thought a condemned man always got to hear the charges being brought against him, you know, corpus delicti."

Wilson brought an open hand down on his desk top rattling the glasses. "Yes, God dammit, everywhere on earth a man has certain rights, but in this damned place they killed people over a cigarette butt!"

"You mean Bory?"

"Bory hell, Pankrac! The bastards hung a woman, the kind of woman who comes along once every hundred years, maybe every five hundred years. And they hid her last letters from her family for over forty years. No decent man can breathe the air here because even the air here is poisoned by the past. And the idea of living here sickens me because it means sharing the same air with the bastards."

"And am I one of the bastards too?"

"Dammit, aren't you the one who told me you can't trust anybody here?"

"And aren't you the one who said to me just days ago in my office, you could tell who to trust?"

"Dammit, just shut up and get out. It was a mistake to come here. I tried to tell that to Sedlacek. But he wouldn't listen. He said I was just the man for this job! What a joke. The right man would have broken her neck by now. I'm not the right man. Coming here was the biggest mistake I've ever made in my life and I've made some big mistakes."

"My mother spent some time in prison."

Wilson raised his eyebrows and glanced at Havlicek who had filled his glass again.

"She received some letters from America and that brought her under suspicion of what they called intrigues against the state. She was given what they called a trial but you know what they were, show trials. It was a kind of quota system with the purpose to terrorize the general population into obedience. I was too young to understand any of it, she sent me to live with a relative under a different name and it stayed that way even after she got out of prison, because children of political prisoners were not allowed to attend universities and she wanted me to have an education."

"You mean your real name isn't Havlicek?"

"No. But I know about the prisons and I know all about Bory. They should tear them down out of respect for those who suffered there."

"You know then about the show trial they had at the theater and the crowd they put there to shout for the blood of three innocent men over a cigarette butt?"

"Yes, I know about it. Everybody does."

"People are nothing but hairless apes and the idea of God creating people in his image is the worst joke imaginable, because no God could create anything so hideous. I never hated anything until I came here. Now I hate so deep I'd like to break someone's neck, if only I had the guts for it. But I'm no better than the rest of the hairless apes. I'm as pitiful and hideous as any of them. I should never have come to this damned place. Everything is poison here."

"I have a photograph that might interest you of an American soldier."

"God dammit, Havlicek, can't you get it, I'm not interested in any American soldiers. I'm just as sick of Americans as I am with Czechs. Because what happened in places like Bory and Pankrac could never have happened without some gutless double crossing son of a bitches who stopped Patton and kissed Stalin's ass. They should have their necks broken too - if there was any justice in this God forsaken world."

"I think this photograph might interest you." Havlicek said and placed the old snapshot on the desk top.

Wilson glanced at it and picked it up. "How the hell did you get this?"

"Do you know him?"

"Hell yes I know him. How the hell did you get this?"

"My mother gave it to me."

"Your mother, don't bull shit me, Havlicek, I'm in no mood for any crap."

"I'm telling you the truth. Take it or leave it."

"Is this your father?"

Havlicek nodded.

Wilson sighed. "Shit! You bastard, you knew all along, didn't you?"

"No. There were thousands of Wilsons in the American Army. I had no proof you were related to this Wilson. I needed proof."

"Why the hell didn't you show me this photograph months ago?"

"There are things you had to learn that no one could tell you. You had to learn them on your own. If you hadn't searched for them then you would never have learned them. And you would never have understood the suffering here. You would know only facts but you knew facts before you came here. But people are more than facts, every life has a story behind it. Like the life of my mother."

"Where is she now?"

"In a graveyard."

"I thought you told me she was in Prague?"

"She is, in a graveyard."

Wilson fell into silence, then looked up. "You know what this means, of course."

"Of course, we're related. Brothers, I guess."

"Half-brothers," Wilson corrected.

"And it means you've got the same loser for a father that I have."

"Like I said, people are more than facts. Your father has a story too. My mother left me a trunk of her keepsakes. I think some of them would interest you. There's some letters."

"From who?"

"From your father. You're welcome to read them, if you would like?"

"I don't see what difference it can make now."

"I think you should read them."

"Do you have a photograph of your mother?"

Havlicek reached into his briefcase. "This is what she looked like when she was nineteen."

Wilson's eyes narrowed as he studied the old snapshot of a young woman with dark hair. There was something about the set of her lips that was familiar. Martina. Wilson rubbed his forehead where a crease had formed. His voice was low. "Thanks, I'd like to see them. Now if you don't mind I think I'd like to be alone for awhile."

Havlicek nodded and closed his briefcase and left the room. He was thoughtful enough to leave his bottle on Wilson's desk.

"Thanks, brother," Wilson murmured after Havlicek had closed the door behind him and reached for the bottle.

Chapter 30

Havlicek laid on Wilson's desk a leather bound photo album. "The letters are inside."
Wilson nodded. "Thanks."
"I'll meet you after school, what time is your last class?"
"I'm finished at three."
"Na shledanou."
"Na shledanou."
When the door closed and Wilson was alone he lifted the front cover of the leather bound album. The first old black and white snapshot was a family posing in front of a Bohemian cottage and he felt he was traveling backward in time. He studied faces without hurry from what must have been grandparents on. It was easy for him to identify the face of Havlicek's mother as a young girl, then as a teen-ager and then a young woman. Her hair was dark, she was pretty without being pretty in a conventional way, intelligent looking without appearing studious or dull. In her eyes as well as expression was a kind of gayness, a delight at being alive, she radiated an optimism that some young people carry into adulthood from youth without having it suppressed by adult realities. Wilson found a poetry in her face that soothed him so he found himself often reluctant to turn the pages. A reality overtook him; he understood why he had liked Havlicek at their first meeting, his eyes had the same quality of intelligence combined with gayness and optimism of his mother's eyes.

He turned the page and found a photograph of Havlicek's mother and an American soldier. Both were young and happy; it was a face of his father that Wilson hadn't known. His father's face was smooth and tanned and in his eyes there was happiness. The face Wilson remembered of his father was of a man who came home after work peaked and tired and who first went to the refrigerator and drank a beer and smoked several cigarettes before he said a pleasant word to anyone. The only thing close to happiness that he could remember of his father was when he had won big at a card game. Then unlike his return from work in the evenings, he would return in a happy mood and making promises about a fishing trip or other promises which he never kept.

But the face of his father in the old snapshots was the face of a happy man, maybe even the face of a man in love. There was no doubt about what the face of Havlicek's mother revealed: she was in love. In every photograph with the American soldier she was not looking into at camera but admiring the face of the man beside her. No man, Wilson speculated, no matter how hard his heart, could fail to respond to the magic of faces that young and happy. It jumped off the photo as mysteriously but as irrepressibly as some old love letters kept the aroma of perfume or flowers long after the perfume had evaporated or the flowers had become brittle fragments.

Wilson found the bundle of letters tied together with a purple ribbon. He had a premonition before he opened the first letter that he would learn information to complicate his life. The letters he read were not eloquent or profound because Wilson's father was neither. But Wilson found in them an essence that love letters possess that give them a timeless appeal: the cry of one human heart that cannot live without another.

Wilson read with sympathy as the date for his father's rotation home came closer. It set in motion the same kind of riveting tightness in his stomach he had when he read Dr. Horakova's last letters. He detected in the choice of words a growing despair as the date came nearer for the soldier to leave.

Then he came to letters with U.S. stamps and postmarks. The postmarks were from Hanford, Washington. The first letter was stamped, January 22, 1946. He wrote about his ride across the Atlantic in a troop ship, his landing at New York, the long train ride across the United States and then his first look at his home town of Hanford. There was no mention of his wife or son, who had been born while he was overseas. The final paragraph expressed his loneliness and longing for the woman he loved.

Wilson thumbed through the bundle of letters with the old American stamps and came to the last letter, postmarked July 17, 1949. He held it for a few moments with a frown and bit his lip as if trying to decide whether he should read it or simply put it back in the bundle with the others and retie the purple ribbon around them. What good could come from reading a man's last letter to a woman he loved when you know the unhappy end? Did it do you any good to read Dr. Horakova's last letter to her husband, her "dear and only boy." Were you better for it, happier, wiser, or larger? No, but you learned something more about the dimensions of the human heart. Wilson opened the last letter.

Dearest Klara:

It's hot here this time of year in the desert, boiling hot. It makes it difficult to sleep even with the air conditioning going full blast and I often wake up during the night. But it's not the heat which stops me from sleeping, it's worry over you. It's been so long since I've received a letter from you. It seems like a hundred years since we were together. Of course, I've read in newspaper stories what has been going on there under the communists and that only makes me worry more.

The only thing I think of day after day is you. Life is empty without you. I get up and I ride my bus out into the desert and put in my time on the atomic project, but I'm thinking of you. Then I come home and eat and try to sleep, but I'm thinking of you. I see your face before me - like a mirage. Did it really happen? Was it all a dream?

I never told you this because I never wanted to add any worry into your life, but I am haunted now by a memory I had as I walked up the gang way of my troop ship in Bremerhaven, the Patch. I felt a kind of terror that told me to run back down the gang way because if not I would never see you again.

But, of course, I didn't. I told myself to take it easy, it was just nerves, I felt the same nerves when the Germans were shooting at us and I survived, so I told myself to settle down and quit worrying. Now I know there was everything to worry about. For without you and the dream of our future life, nothing has any meaning to me. I can't imagine living without you. It's almost four years since I've seen you and still not a particle of my feelings for you have changed - they only grow deeper with time.

I am not a religious man, you know, and never have been, but for these last months I begin to learn how to pray. I don't pray that we should be together again, I don't ask for the moon. I only pray that I'll get a scrap of paper in the mail from you telling me that you are okay. That's all I ask for. But it never comes. It's like I am on Mars. I feel cut off from life itself. It goes on day after day and I think I can't stand it another day because the ache inside doesn't lessen but hurts a little more until my whole body seems to ache. I think my heart will stop.

I've discovered there are no pills to cure it. I've discovered there is nothing that helps. I've tried everything. One day simply follows another. I wonder how long it can go on before something inside me breaks for good?

I must go now as my ride to the bus depot is honking his horn for me outside. I pray only for a scrap of paper when I get home with your name on it.

                Love,
                Your Harry

Lost in a mist of thoughts Wilson sat staring at the paper he held. His mind seemed froze and it was some time before he managed to fold the letter and slide it back into its envelope.

She was probably already in detention, he considered, or they were screening her mail coming in and stopping her's from going out. She was probably going through the same kind of slow death as his father. The communists killed many people, some with bullets, some with the guillotine, some with the hangman's rope, some with the interrogator's club. But maybe no death was worse than the death to lovers who died out of forced separation and worry until everything inside them was dead.

A scrap of paper was all he wanted. A miserable scrap of paper. And it never came. The bastards killed him too. They killed everything decent and good and gentle like a plague and no one will ever know how much damage they did to the human race in less than a century.

The old man, Wilson understood, never told anyone. He kept it all inside. Maybe it started harmless enough. Maybe they met at one of those street dances he saw photographs of American soldiers dancing with Czech girls. Maybe things started innocent and seemed harmless. Love can happen that way. You innocently look into someone's eyes...then. Remember how you first looked at Martina. It was so innocent you hardly noticed her. You never meant anything to happen and what happened after that could have happened if you had a wife. Being married would not have made any difference because you fought against it as hard as you could. The old man was right when he wrote there are no pills to cure it, there is nothing to cure it, not once it starts. So it's no good to think or imagine any longer you're better than he was. Nothing helped him and nothing can help you because what happens between a man and woman has its own gravity that once started there can be no escape from. It levels everyone, the mighty and the weak to one miserable condition.

But what a unique woman the old man met. Havlicek's mother might have only been nineteen, but there was a depth to her that came off the photographs. Her face had a blend of gentleness and intelligence of an older woman who comprehended what was worldly, yet her eyes still reflected something girlish and optimistic that some call innocence. And isn't that really what a man loves in a woman: the idea he can find in her goodness and gentleness and sensitivity he could find in no other woman? Isn't that the gravity that pulls you toward Martina?

Wilson remembered Havlicek's words. "You know only facts, but people aren't facts. Every person has a story behind them. Like my mother. Like your father."

But where do any of life's contradictions ever lead to? It seemed life was only one old tragedy played out over and over down through the centuries with only different names and places in them. And what good were the unwritten higher laws the Greeks wrote about that men had a duty to obey? To what purpose was it to obey unwritten laws if a man never found any order in the world that he had to live in day by day?

One reality was clear that had little to do with an unwritten higher law; there was a duty to tell his father he had a third son -if he was still alive. That meant someone had to search for him. And there was only one person left to do it, welcome home, brother.

Chapter 31

The grass in front of the school of economics was green and the trees were dressed out with leaves on their branches. The first real breath of summer had arrived. Wilson sat on the bench in front of the school waiting for Martina Bellekova. He felt a sense of anticipation waiting for her, as he always did. He thought with time it would pass, but it never did. He scanned the tops of the heads of the passengers getting off the streetcar on Klatovska Street looking for her dark hair in the evening twilight. He spotted her walking toward him, somewhat shyly, as she always did. Perhaps, Wilson wondered, she was also feeling uncertain and nervous. A nice couple. Full of confidence.

He smiled politely as she sat down on the bench next to him, but not too close. "It's warm and very pleasant tonight, like real summer."

"Yes," she agreed, "it feels like summer has arrived at last."

"You look nice tonight."

She glanced at him and smiled as if disbelieving his compliment, as always. "It seems like you're wearing your hair differently?"

She smiled. "Yes, a little."

"I notice when you wear it different, I notice even when you change the color of your nails."

"Really?" she blushed.

"Really. Did you receive my letter yesterday?"

"Yes, thank you. I sent you an answer."

"Most of the time when I get your letters I wait until after school and take them over to the gril and read them with a glass of wine. Then I write an answer to you in my notebook with some wine."

"Do you ever read my letters more than once?"
"I always read them more than once."
"How many times?"
"Many."
"Probably not as many times as I read your letters."
"Come on, my letters must be boring?"
"Not for me. I take them with me to work to read on my lunch break and then I read them again on the bus home. I think letters are the most beautiful thing a person can give or get from another person, don't you?"

Wilson took his time to answer. "I guess it depends on the conditions. Letters have a way of freezing time so you can always go back to it. Not long ago I read some letters my father wrote to a woman when he was a soldier. And after I read his letters I felt like I was alive in his time. It was a strange, almost unpleasant feeling."

"Who did he write the letters to?"
"To a woman in Plzen."
"That is strange, who was she?"
Wilson hesitated. "Havlicek's mother."
"Your father knew Roman's mother?"
Wilson nodded.
"How is it possible?"
"There are somethings I've been wanting to tell you."
"What, that you're going home this summer after school is out?"
"Yes, I'm planning to go home this summer. I have to find my father and tell him that he has a son in Plzen."
"But doesn't he already know you're here?"
"No, but I have to tell him he has another son in Plzen..."
"Please, you don't have to make up a story for me. I can understand if you want to leave. I've been expecting it."
"Listen to me, Roman Havlicek is my brother, my half-brother. Do you understand my father is the same as his. It's not a story."

Martina Bellekova ran the finger tips of one hand through the ends of her hair. "This is strange, almost too strange to believe."

"Life is strange."

"You don't need an excuse to leave, you know."

"I don't want to leave. I have to do this. It's a duty."

"I told you, I've been expecting it."

"It's only for a few weeks, maybe a couple of months and then I'll be back."

"You don't have to give me excuses, you're free to do as you please."

"You're not listening to me, why don't you come with me?"

She glanced at him and smiled weakly. "Why should I want to do that?"

"Because I'd like you to come with me."

"That's silly, we don't know each other well enough for that kind of thing."

"The only thing that really matters is how much people care about each other and I care enough to know I need you with me."

"But people say you have other girlfriends in Plzen."

"I don't have any girlfriends in Plzen. I never have. Not since I met you."

"I'm not sure I believe you. I've heard talk about you and other women. People have seen you with them."

"You can't stop people from talking, but I don't care what they say. I know how it's been with me since I met you."

"I don't understand you."

"Maybe it's not necessary to understand someone. There are lots of things I don't understand in life, but if they're true, then they're true."

"What's true about us?"

"What's true is I care about you more than anyone and have since the time I first saw you."

"I wish it was true."

"Stop it, I just said it's true."

"But why me, I don't think I'm beautiful - "

"But I think you're beautiful and that's all that matters, isn't it?"

"Who can believe a man? I'm sure there must be a woman in Plzen who is disappointed because she believed in you."

"I did get involved with a woman, but it was because you wouldn't give our relationship a chance. I got tired of running into walls. Maybe a stronger man than me wouldn't have done it."

"I pity her."

"People get over those kind of things."

"Maybe not, some people never get over them. Were there other women you got involved with?"

Wilson glanced at her and nodded.

"How many?"

"What difference does it make?"

"How many?"

"More than one."

She turned away and became silent and Wilson felt her retreating behind a wall. "I said I was sorry."

"Believe me, I'll never let it happen to me."

"Will you come with me?"

"No. You might change your mind once you're home. I think it's better to never know something than to know it and then lose it."

"Don't you believe me, I need you."

"Where does your father live?"

"I don't know."

"How can you not know where your father is?"

"He and my mother divorced when I was a boy and he dropped out of sight."

"Then maybe he's dead now?"

"I've thought of that. But I have to try and find him. Someone has to tell him about Roman."

"Did he love Havlicek's mother or only sleep with her like some American soldiers did with Czech women?"

Wilson ignored the sarcasm. "He loved her as much as a man can love a woman."

"How can you be so sure?"

"It was in his letters. And I believe it."

"Men say things in letters that aren't true."

"When I was a boy I thought he was a bad man for leaving us. Maybe I even hated him. But now I know he wasn't a bad man. He just loved a woman so much that it destroyed him. I think it would have been better if someone would have shot him."

"How can you say such a thing?"

"Because without her something necessary in him died. He couldn't survive without her. Havlicek's mother went to prison for getting letters from an American soldier. It destroyed both their lives."

"Tell me more about them."

"My father was already married when he met her. I'm sure if it was not for us he would have come back to try and help her. He didn't know she was pregnant. He sent her some money to get out of here, but after the elections in forty-six I guess it was hard to get papers to leave. And how many people right after the war could imagine that the communists would take over?"

"Have you seen a photograph of Havlicek's mother?"

"Yes."

"What did she look like?"

"She was pretty, she reminded me of you."

"Are you making up another story?"

"I'm not, it's true, all of it."

"But it seems like a story, like something out of a book. What did your father look like?"

"Something like me, I guess, or maybe I look a little like him." She glanced at Wilson. "You had a wife too, didn't you?"

"Yes, I told you about her in a letter."

"You only mentioned her, did you love her?"

"I thought I did in the beginning."

"What changed your mind?"

"I don't know. Who knows about love?"

"No one, I think."

"But what I feel about you is different than what I felt about her."

"How is it different?"

"I was younger then."

"What difference does that make?"

"It makes a great difference. I've had a long time to think about things like love or what people say is love. And I've had enough time to learn what makes me happy and the things that don't make me happy. I've learned there are things you can't know until you experience them. No one can tell them to you. You just have to live them to know them. So now I know them. And I know what I feel about you is different than what I've felt about any other woman."

"Why should I believe you when you say you don't know anything about love?"

"I think I wrote to you once I don't believe in using the word love until you've earned the right to use it, but it's true that I don't know anything about love. I only know that what you feel about a person changes with time. So you have to be careful about using words. The best thing is to show people how you feel."

"I'm not sure about love either. My younger sister has already been married and divorced once. I remember how she said she loved this man before they were married. Now she can't stand him. And I've had other friends go through the same thing. What's important for me is for a man to be here everyday when I need him, to bring me flowers, to write me letters, but most of all to be here everyday. I wonder if you have the patience for those kind of things. I've heard how you play basketball and how you coach the boys at basketball. You haven't much patience."

"No, it's a weakness of mine."

"Won't it take some patience to find your father?"

"Yes, I'm sure of that. But you must understand I'd rather stay here, but I've got to do it."

"I understand it, so do your duty, as you call it, and then come back when you're sure about everything. But I can't come with you. Some women feel deeper than you can imagine and suffer deeper than you imagine. So they have to be careful who they get involved with."

"I've always believed that you felt deeper than other women."

"Well go do what you feel you have to and come back when you're sure what it is that you want."

"I'm sure of what I want now and I don't want to wait and end up like my father."

"I thought you said you didn't know where he is, so how can you know how he ended up?"

"I can imagine how he ended up."

"What do you imagine?"

"Do you know what a derelict is?"

"No I'm not sure of it."

"It's someone who has no home, no family, no steady job, no faith, in short a derelict is someone who is a kind of walking dead man. Usually a drunk too. They live in places called flop houses."

"What are flop houses?"

"They're cheap hotels in the bad parts of big cities where derelicts live. They are the saddest place in the world, I think, because they are warehouses for the people no one else wants - like my old man."

"Maybe you'll be surprised and find him living a normal life."

"That would surprise me. The man in America who asked me to come here to work said I was in danger of becoming a derelict. I laughed when he told me that, but maybe he was right. Maybe I was becoming like my old man. I tried for a long time to harden myself because I believed if I became hard enough then I could survive anything and I would never end up like my father."

"I don't understand, what was it that you were trying to harden yourself against?"

"After my brother and mother died all I could see in the world was chaos."

"I've wondered, we once talked about God and you said the jury was out for you. Is the jury still out?"

"Why do you ask?"

"Well you admit now after all the years of thinking your father was a bad man you were wrong, maybe now you see other things differently too or do you still see only chaos."

"Living here I've found almost everything I used to believe was true but only half true. So I guess the jury is still out about God because I've seen here that there is more suffering than I ever imagined in this world. I've seen how life really is more complicated than I imagined. I've seen how the fate of a human being can turn on nothing more than a cigarette butt or a scrap of paper. My father, for example, waited month after month for a letter to keep him alive, but it never came. Somehow I feel shamed by what I've found here, because it involves me too. No one can say they aren't involved just because they happened to live somewhere else when evil happened. Because the cruelty people here inflicted on other people only tell us about ourselves. It seems to me that the more one learns about people the less he can believe in anything in the world."

"Perhaps that's because you expect people to be like you?"

"What do you mean, like me?"

Martina Bellekova smiled and out of habit ran some finger tips through her hair. "The first time I saw you when you came to our class with Roman, I felt a kind of energy about you that was stronger than anyone elses. I think the others must have felt it too. That kind of energy gives you a certain advantage over other people. So maybe people with normal energy disappoint you, maybe I disappoint you too because in some ways I'm ordinary. You probably didn't even notice me in class that first time, did you?"

"I noticed you," Wilson said after a silence, but his silence allowed her the point.

"Yet you want me now to follow you to America on blind faith. But I haven't blind faith. I don't know how you can expect it of me. You have so much energy I imagine that you throw yourself at things in life without fear of the risks, then if life or people disappoint you and you no longer find them interesting you move on to the next risk. A woman learns early enough that one of her greatest attractions to men is her mystery, but that doesn't last long in life. You mention pain you felt when I wouldn't tell you about my feelings and private life, but when there is a great feeling for one person from another there is also a potential for great suffering. You can't believe it, I'm sure, but I feel like I've already died a hundred times for you by wondering if the moment will come that you change your mind about me or if you will simply leave Plzen and go back to America. I think it's much better to die just once than care for someone so deeply you die a hundred times by imagining them leaving you. I've already died a hundred times for you and you don't even know it."

"Maybe so," Wilson whispered. "But if you've died a hundred times for me, then you're still behind me, because I feel like I've died a thousand and one times for you. Maybe you can't believe it, but I know a little bit about suffering."

Chapter 32

It was a Saturday morning basketball game that Wilson had played countless times before in a park as a boy. But this basketball game was in Plzen and everyone else was still a boy, except him. It was Wilson and Robert and Sedlacek against three slightly older and larger boys, who played on the Lokomotiva men's team.

The games were played until one side reached fifty and then a new game began. Wilson didn't want to be the one to suggest they stop and he worked harder than Robert and Sedlacek. His habit was constant motion and pressure. It was the way he was taught to play and the only way he knew how. Every game for him, even a pick up game on a Saturday morning in a park, was a challenge, as much against himself as the opponent.

"Keep moving, we'll wear them down, keep moving," he encouraged Robert and Sedlacek more than once when he sensed they were giving in to fatigue. And they did. Afterward Wilson felt exhausted, but the sweetness of winning, even in a meaningless Saturday morning game in a park, left him feeling jaunty.

He smiled as they sat on a bench cooling off and toweling away the sweat which trickled down their foreheads around their eyes. "Sometimes we used to play all day when I was about your age. Often in the summer the temperature in the desert would climb to a hundred, but we kept on playing. We were afraid to be the ones to quit."

"All day?" Robert asked skeptically.

Wilson nodded and paused to mop up some sweat around his neck. "We would get as brown as Indians during the summer and if the game happened to be against boys from another high school in our city it became a question of honor; no matter how hot it was you couldn't quit. And above all you couldn't lose. We played in a park by a river because it had the best baskets and nets. Most of the baskets in the park had the nets worn out but this court had good baskets and a cement floor that was smooth without cracks and on Saturday mornings in the summer boys from all over the city and outside the city would come. It was like a tournament. You kept playing until you lost twice. Then by late afternoon the two best teams would play for the championship. I've seen boys pass out on the court because they lost so much sweat they were dehydrated. And by noon the cement reflected the heat so it was hotter on the court than off it. But we never wanted to quit or lose in our neighborhood, it was a question of pride,I guess it still is."

"Is that why you play so hard?"

"You never want to lose being able to challenge yourself to reach a goal."

"Our basketball team has terrible habits, haven't we?"

Wilson smiled knowing he couldn't avoid the truth. "Yes."

"It hurt you to watch us play, didn't it?"

"Yes, it was painful to watch us play without some passion."

"Is it possible if we had better habits we could win a championship?"

Wilson became thoughtful as he considered each player on the team. "Yes, it's possible. We need one more boy to play opposite you with more size and who will play defense. That's all. Our players are big enough and they are quick enough. They just need to learn new habits."

"I've heard you're going to America this summer?"

"Yes, I have to find my father, it's my duty."

"Will you come back?"

"I'm planning to come back."

"Do you really want to come back?"

"Yes, very much."

"I've heard you aren't happy here and are glad to leave."

"It's not true. I want you to know that because many things can happen in life that you can't plan on and afterward people say things that aren't true about you. The truth is I want to come back and coach basketball again next season and someday I want to win a championship here in Plzen."

"I've heard there are problems at your school and some people don't want you back next year."

Wilson smiled and ran his towel over his face where sweat had beaded up again on his forehead, around his eyes and the back of his neck. "There are some problems at my school. I'm not an easy teacher. I teach a little like I coach basketball. I want my students to perform at a certain level because I want them to have something to take with them for the rest of their lives when they leave my class at the end of the year. And at my school they have some old habits that are hard to get rid of and many people don't want to change, just as some of the older boys on the team didn't want to change. So maybe I'll teach at a new school. But I'm telling the truth, I want to come back."

"Have you ever wanted a son?" Robert asked.

Wilson turned to study the boy because he heard something deep and sincere in his voice. "Yes, I think most every man dreams at one time about having a son. I'm the same as most every man."

"Do you still have that dream?"

"Maybe it comes to me now and then."

"I think if a boy had a father like you he would be lucky."

"Thank you. I think if a man had a son like you he would be lucky too."

They lapsed into awkward silence.

"How's your father?" Wilson asked to break up the silence.

"I haven't seen him for awhile, he travels a lot for his work and he spends a lot of time with his girlfriend."

Wilson nodded. "How's your mother?"

"Good. Can you tell me why you never had a son?"

Wilson swatted at a flying insect with his towel and took a deep breath. "Sure. I never met the right woman."
"What was the matter with your wife?"
"Nothing. It's a question of chemistry between people, something like it is with a basketball team. If the right chemistry isn't there, then it goes wrong. What goes on between a man and a woman is very delicate and I've never met the right woman."
"I've heard you have a girlfriend."
"Maybe so. Maybe not. There's a woman here I care about."
"She must be beautiful."
"Maybe not to everyone, but she is to me."
"Will you marry her?"
"If I had the chance I guess I would."
"Then you'd take her to America to live."
"No. Why would I want to do that, don't you believe me that I'm coming back because I like it here?"
Robert began bouncing his basketball and avoiding Wilson's eyes. "Oh, everyone knows we are poor and backward here and it will be many years before we can live like other Western countries. And it will never be like America here."
"Robert, listen to me carefully. I love my country because I was born there and you have to learn to love your country too, maybe not for what it is today or yesterday but for what it can be in the future. Maybe we won't win a championship here at Lokomotiva, but think of a time when you might be the coach after me. You can teach boys here good habits and how to win. Think of all the good things that can be here when you're as old as me, then you'll have children. Don't try to be like other countries, because you never can be. Just try to make what you have better and more human. Believe me something good can be made right here, right here in old Plzen. I've seen many places in the world and I know something good can be made right here, do you know how I know?"
"How?"

"These old buildings. Some of these old buildings in Plzen are as beautiful as any buildings in the world. They're dirty now, but once they were clean and beautiful and someone had to design them and build them according to their imagination and dreams. That means there was something good here. The president of France said, 'A country with great architecture is a great country.' Much has been lost here under the communists because of bad education and laziness that comes from political corruption. But the goodness that was here before them can't be destroyed completely. So I know something good can be built here. Believe me, Robert, it can be. I know it's hard for you to see it, but you have to believe it because this is the only country you're ever going to be born to just as you can be born only from one woman."

Robert quit bouncing his basketball and sat down again beside his coach. Wilson waited for him to speak. He felt the boy thinking over his words.

"But if you don't come back, it would never be the same again. We would go back to the old ways. Do you remember the time after practice when you asked us why we thought we lost and Sedlacek said, 'because it is in us.' That's what everybody thinks. No one really believes we will ever be any different. Not our team, not Plzen, not Czechoslovakia. We are poor because it is in us, they think. If you don't come back, people will say, see he was unhappy here because we are a backward place and always will be backward."

"Then they'd be wrong. This will be a beautiful city someday whether I'm here or not. Believe me."

"I want to."

"Then believe me when I say I'm coming back. There is only one thing that could stop me."

"What?"

"The thing that stops everyone sooner or later; death. No one knows when it's their time to die. We always think we have more time than we do. As we grow older we learn that too. So I've learned to try to do the best I can in everything for today. And even if my time came to die this summer you would have some good memories of this time to keep the rest of your life and you'll understand when you're as old as me that the best things a man ever has in life are his memories. Believe me."

"You'll come back, won't you."

"Of course I will."

"You're too young to die or something like that."

"Don't believe that. No one is ever too young to die and no one is ever too old to find happiness. My brother died when he was much younger than I am. And I knew soldiers in Vietnam who died even younger. And some very good people died here under the Germans and then under the communists who could have helped make this a beautiful country it once was. So the truth is I'm very lucky to have lived this long and been able to be here and know you and see these old buildings and know Martina."

"Her name is Martina?"

"Yes."

"Do you really love her?"

"Be careful with the word love. I've heard people say they love their dog or their job or even their automobile. But love is something a person should be ready to die for. How many people would die for their dog or their job or their automobile?"

"So you don't love her?"

Wilson smiled. "I never said that. I think I care about her as much as any man cares for any woman. And I think I would die for her if I had to. But I've never had to, so I guess I haven't the right to use it yet."

"What is it like loving someone then, like you love Martina?"

Wilson smiled again. "You'll learn that too."

"But what is it like?"

"Oh, maybe there aren't any words for it, but a lot of the time you feel like dying."

"That sounds awful, how can love be like dying?"

"Well, sometimes love is awful, when something is deep enough, there is pain to it. Like wanting to be a champion, if it goes deep enough the pain from losing is awful."

"I'm not sure I ever want to love a woman."

Wilson bit his lip so as not to smile. "Oh, you will. You surely will learn someday all about loving and dying and how you can't have the one without the other, if it's worth anything."

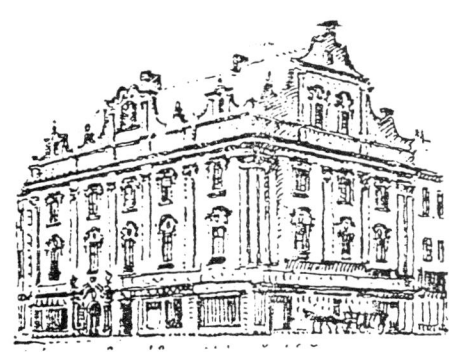

Chapter 33

It was an easy land to love, Wilson thought, as he hiked beside Roman Havlicek on the shoulder of the country road. In the distance as far as he could see in any direction were rolling hills shadowed with dark forests. On the flanks of the hills were fields of grain, brown and ripe in the morning sun.

When they passed through a village dogs barked and fat hens and roosters strutted in the streets. Every village had an old church, most often a creme color, with a single belfry and onion shaped dome. The villages must have been exactly the same a hundred years before or even two hundred years ago, he thought. It was calm and the pleasant strain of his back pack and the sound of the gravel against the soles of his boots soothed him so that it was easy to fall into his private thoughts.

It was wonderful country, but how long could it stay that way? He had seen streams Germans in RVs and campers pass through Plzen and how long would it be before Czechs could also afford such vehicles to invade the countryside as Americans did on the weekends in America? No place is immune from modern life. There would be satellite dishes in the villages and farm houses, just as in America. You have to enjoy whatever is natural and good while you have it and make it a good memory before it changes, he thought. Things change quickly. All things change quickly.

A memory came to Wilson of the same kind of Saturday morning when he was a boy and he and Phil had gotten up early and hiked out into the desert to rock hunt. They wore cowboy hats and boots, canteens, carried lunches of peanut butter sandwiches and took a compass, though they didn't need it, of course. They had to skirt around the security check posts and hike close to the Yakima River. Ahead of them was the great bulge of the Rattlesnake Mountains. Wilson had always imagined a great Indian camp had been there in the past. The Yakima Indians still had fishing rights to fish year round on the river with nets and they often saw Indians on their hikes, fishing in the mornings from their wooden platforms they had built in the currents of the river.

Sometimes a white tailed dear would be spooked and dash from behind a shoulder high clump of sage into the open. Jackrabbits would be flushed and run zig zag fashion through the undergrowth. And it was a game with them to warn each other to be careful not to stumble over a rattlesnake. Sometimes, of course, they did actually come across a rattler and if they had a club with them they would kill it, which they would talk about for weeks as the great battle with the monster snake. Because in memory rattlesnakes always became larger than in life. And there was always the pleasant sound of a horned owl cooing.

It was a good place to be a boy, Wilson thought, with a smile. They imagined themselves to be cowboys and the desert filled with hostile Indians and dangerous animals. The danger instead came from radiation they couldn't see. All the innocence of that time seemed more than a lifetime ago.

They had climbed to the top of a hill and it revealed a village with its church steeple and tiled rooftops at the bottom of the slope nestled between hills. Wilson saw the trace of a stream that cut into the center of the village and wound its way out of sight.

The sign at the village entrance read, Mladotice. A dog began barking and soon they came to a village pub.

"Ready for a break?" Havlicek asked.

Wilson nodded. There were benches outside the pub and they strode to the benches and slipped out of their shoulder harnesses. They sat on the flat benches with their backs against the pub wall and the morning sun warming their faces. Wilson heard the coo of a bird and wondered if it was a barn owl. The sun made him feel lazy.

"I've been thinking about something for the last couple of weeks Roman."

"What?"

"I've been thinking about a plan for the summer for me and you. I've got a car at home that we could use to look for the old man, then when we're ready to come home, we'll sell the car to pay for our tickets. What do you think?"

"I think you're asking the wrong person."

"What do you mean?"

"You should be asking Martina."

"I already have, but she didn't think it was such a good plan."

"Maybe you asked the wrong question. Maybe she was hoping for something with more of a future to it, not just a vacation."

"Maybe. But right now I'm not in a position to offer anyone any future until I look for the old man. I tried to tell her it was a duty, but I don't know if she understood. But I know that you understand and I think if the old man is alive and we found him, it would mean a lot to him to see you and hear about your mother."

Havlicek took a long drink of water from his canteen. Wilson saw a smile building around his lips and the familiar mischievous light come into his eyes. "Well, that's something to think about."

"What's there to think about? It's got to be done. It's my duty, that's for sure, but I guess it's partly your duty too. And there are some things you can't put off, when the time comes to do them you've got to do it or the chance never comes again."

"I know," Havlicek answered with a sigh.

"This is easy country to love because it seems to me it must have been about the same a hundred or even two hundred years ago. It's peaceful and natural and you can feel the old rhythm of life here. This is the real Bohemia, I think."

Wilson paused to take a drink from his canteen. "But all things change, that's what I learned in America. I was thinking this morning about the desert where Phil and I used to hike on mornings like these. I couldn't imagine then how the desert would change. Nobody could. Now there are buildings everywhere, fruit orchards, people in their campers and recreation vehicles parked in the most remote places. The peacefulness of the desert is gone forever. And boys today will never know it like we did and have their imaginations developed in the ways ours were. But I'd still like you to see that desert or what's left of it."

Havlicek grinned. "I've saved money year after year for a journey to America, never really believing I'd ever set foot on American soil. Then the revolution came."

Havlicek took a drink of water and they listened to a rooster crow. A plump calico cat edged around the corner and sat watching them. Up the street a housewife had opened the windows of her bedroom on the second floor and hung a feather blanket out to air. Wilson watched a boy pounding a tennis ball against the side of a building. The calmness of the village settled into him.

"And?" he asked as he watched the boy stroking the tennis ball against the wall.

"And I began to dream for the first time in years of really going to America."

"Where in America?"

"I dreamed I'd somehow find my father. You know, something improbable and unrealistic. Then you came."

"Tell me the truth, the absolute truth. You knew almost from the first time we met who my father was, didn't you?"

Havlicek took another drink of water and wiped his lips. "No, to be absolutely honest. You've read his letters and there was no mention of a wife or son. And I knew Wilson is a common American name. But all the circumstances gave me hope and I started dreaming about things I never dared to dream."

"But I was from the same state, why didn't you tell me in the beginning and show me the photographs?"

"From what you told me about your father and because you were American, I knew there was much you had to learn on your own."

"That seems to me pretty cold."

"Maybe, but necessary. You know there are things in life that must be learned on your own, no one can tell them to you. I knew I could always show you the photographs. But you were convinced your father was a bad man. I wanted you to learn about life here under the communists, how everything became so inhuman that it touched nearly everyone in ways no one can understand unless they were here."

"I'll admit it seems to me everything I believed before I came here has been turned upside down. I wasn't sure of much before

I came and now I'm not sure of anything."

"But now you know your father wasn't a bad man."

Wilson nodded. "I guess, he was just a man who got caught in the wrong place at the wrong time. He met a beautiful woman and his life began coming apart. Learning about his life it makes me wonder if we can really ever know another person in this world."

"Everyone has a hundred sides, I think. If we get to know twenty percent of their sides we're lucky and that can take a lifetime."

"You know, I'd really like to find the old buzzard, if it's possible."

"But now you know he isn't a buzzard," Havlicek added.

Wilson nodded. "Where to now?"

"Manetin," Havlicek said standing up. "We'll take a lunch break there, then head south to Plasy. In Plasy we can hop a train to Plzen, if we feel like it."

They shouldered back into their backpacks and stopped at a well with a hand pump at the edge of the village to fill their canteens. Soon they were hiking again in silence, the sound of gravel under foot, the pleasant strain of their packs and the sight of the rolling fields of grain easing them into private reflections. The sun climbed higher and grew warmer. Wilson felt sweat collecting across his forehead and on the back of his neck when they hiked up the grade of a long hill.

The landscape was dotted with farm houses. A cluster of houses would appear in the distance and they would pass through a village serenaded by the baying of village dogs. At Manetin they broke for lunch under the shade of an apple tree. They ate cheese and salami and drank bottles of Plzner beer. Then they were up and into their packs heading south toward Plasy. By late afternoon a single church tower in Plasy came into view. At the edge of the town Roman Havlicek said, "There's something here I'd like to show you."

202 A HOME IN BOHEMIA

Wilson nodded. "I hope there's a pub open here, I'm a little dry." Havlicek guided Wilson to a graveyard behind a church. Many of the headstones carried the traditional photograph of the deceased. Havlicek stopped in front of a stone with a photograph of a face Wilson recognized. Havlicek's mother.

KLARA KOZELOVA
APRIL 20, 1926
DECEMBER 18, 1989

"I don't understand, I thought you said your mother was buried in Prague?"
"She is and she isn't. I had two mothers in life. My mother's

sister, who I grew up with and my real mother, who is buried here. My mother's sister, an older sister, married a man named Havlicek and they had a son who died named Roman. I took his name and birth certificate."

"What's your real name?"

"I feel my real name is Roman Havlicek. I've never been called anything else. But my mother named me Karel."

Wilson stood looking at Havlicek trying to imagine him as Karel Kozel. He decided he liked him better as Roman Havlicek. "She lived long enough to see the revolution."

Havlicek's smile was one of satisfaction. "I think somehow she always hoped for it. She died suddenly, there was no long illness or complications. She just died in her sleep one night. They said it was her heart, but it seems to me the revolution freed her."

"Did you see her after the revolution?"

"Oh sure, I saw her often before the revolution. Most people thought she was only my aunt."

"When did she give you the letters and photographs?"

"A few weeks before she died. We had a long talk and she told me everything about her life. She never asked me to, but I think she hoped someday I'd go to America and find him."

"Didn't she ever get married?"

"No."

Wilson took a long look at the photograph on the headstone of the face he had come to admire. He left Havlicek alone with his thoughts and waited for him by the church. Looking at the photograph he'd felt a tightness in his stomach, the same kind he got when reading about political prisoners.

When Havlicek came they walked silently toward the center of town to find a pub. Inside they sat over their beer, each man reluctant to break into the others silence.

"Don't be angry, I can see when you're angry," Havlicek finally said. "She kept faith with what she believed in. She loved a man and she never compromised it. Maybe she even knew that you would come someday."

"Havlicek, don't give me any of your philosophy crap, I'm not in the mood for it. They killed her. You know it. They killed her and they killed my old man at the same time. There's not a chance in a million we'll find him alive - but you're coming with me, even if I have to kidnap you?"

Roman Havlicek smiled. "Of course, I'm coming. It's my duty, isn't it?"

Wilson allowed himself a smile.

"Now admit it, David, can't you see something of grace in what you've learned. Something much larger and important than the suffering was?"

"Grace! It wasn't grace but you who left the book about Horakova and the letter from the political prisoner on my desk, wasn't it?"

"Of course, I could see you were getting discouraged. You needed some encouragement and hope. So I visited a woman who had been in prison with my mother and we fixed a package for you."

"I knew it, I knew it had to be you."

Roman Havlicek reached into his backpack and handed Wilson a thin little book. "Here, I think you've been looking for this."

Wilson picked up the little book, *First Love,* by Ivan Turgenev. He frowned. He'd almost forgotten his request of Havlicek and never really expected to find a copy of it.

"It's a wonderful story, terribly Russian. I read it years ago when I was a student at the university. Poor Zenaida, poor Vladimir."

Hearing the names of Zinaida and Vladimir for Wilson was a trigger, like hearing the first strains of an old melody, that released a string of memories in flashes, the last flash was the book's ending. He turned to the book's final page and scanned the lines.

"Why did you want this particular book?"

Wilson looked up with a crease across his forehead "A friend of mine in Russian asked me to remember Turgenev's last words we'd once talked about. And I couldn't."

"And now?"

Wilson smiled, but his frown remained. "I remember now."

"What is it that comes back to you?"

Wilson bit his lip. "Where did you get this book?" he asked in a tone of voice which couldn't mask his discomfort.

"In a book store of course."

"But this is an English version. You sent a letter to England, didn't you?"

"Maybe, what's the difference where I got it. It's a wonderful story told in a Russia style. What did you talk to your Russian friend about?"

"You're hopeless, Havlicek, absolutely hopeless. If you think this is a wonderful story then it's hopeless."

"No, I'm hopeful, absolutely hopeful. You're avoiding my question, what was it you're friend asked you to remember?"

"Death," Wilson said almost under breath.

"Death?"

Wilson opened up the book and read. "*What has come of it all - of all that I had hoped for? What have I left that is fresher, dearer to me, than the memories of that brief storm, that one morning in the spring? But even then, in those light-hearted days of youth, I did not close my eyes to the voice which called to me, which came to me from beyond the grave.*" Wilson closed the book and set it back down on the table.

"And what did you talk about with your friend?"

"She talked, I listened."

"Tell me what she said."

"You're hopeless, she's hopeless."

"You're avoiding the issue."

Wilson hesitated as he remembered Klara Kozelova's grave they had visited a few minutes ago. "It's hopeless to talk about it, Havlicek."

"What's hopeless?"

"Life."

"What do you mean?"

"Can't you see it? He knew it when he got on the troop ship in Bremerhaven that he was doomed. You read his last letter to your mother. No matter what he did he knew someone would suffer. Life is only about suffering."

"No there is something greater than suffering. Something called grace."

"You're hopeless."

"What did your friend say about it?"

"I told you she's as hopeless as you."

"What did she say?"

"She believes in spirits, spirits of the dead. She believes they guide us."

"Nonsense isn't it. Rubbish, I mean she probably even believes in such things as souls. She's hopeless. Absolutely hopeless," Havlicek said mimicking Wilson.

Wilson shot Havlicek a glance from under pinched brows. "Knock off the crap, Roman. I don't believe in any of it."

"Of course not. You just came here by accident, walked into my school, met me, met Martina, all by accident. But there's no grace to it, it's all accident."

"What difference does it make how I got here, your mother is dead, my father is dead. Horakova is dead. Phil is dead."

"Well, first of all we don't know your father is dead. And second, what do you suppose your father or Phil or my mother or even Milada Horakova would say to you if they were in this room? Go back, give up, or stay here, fight for something, build something, believe in something. What do you think they'd say to you?"

"I haven't any idea."

Havlicek beamed. "Oh, you can do better than that. The truth is that inside you now you're not sure of anything because now you know everything is possible. When you came here you believed your father was an evil person, a loser, but you learned he was just the opposite and that he had noble instincts. I doubt you had any hope of meeting a woman you could really care deeply about, like Martina. And of course the last person you ever imagined finding was a brother. You know very well that if they were alive they would tell you there is something much larger than suffering, the gift of grace. But you have to accept it and reject the idea of suffering."

"You're impossible, you know. And hopeless. What am I going to do with you? How am I going to go through life with a brother like you?"

"I don't know David, I was wondering how I was going to go through life with a brother like you!"

Wilson looked into Havlicek's eyes, but he saw the same eyes and expression that he saw in the photograph of his mother. He was right, Wilson thought, he was no longer sure of what was possible or not possible. Bohemia had turned everything upside down in his life.

"I guess," Wilson said with a sigh, but with a relenting smile, "we're going to have to learn to suffer with each other."

"No," Havlicek answered, "we're going to have to learn to live with each other and the idea of grace."

Outside the Boar's Head *hostinec* in Plasy the sun dropped behind the round hills of Bohemia and turned the western sky a deep orange which silhouetted the hills dark against the horizon. A village dog howled, an owl hooted and the faint refrains of men singing an old Bohemian song carried over the evening air into the village streets.

Discover why some critics declare "Roger Burke is the most important American writer today."

Beyond Their Country
(1976) 253 pg. $10

The Last Cowboy
(1989) 273 pg. $10

We have acquired a limited number of books written by Roger Burke. These are authentic, unabridged and unaltered first editions. Collectors can order at:

        Columbia River Book Co.
        3404 S. Auburn
        Kennewick, Wash. 99337
        tel: (509) 582-3953

These books are the first published works of an American writer who is entirely different and unique from any other modern writer. No modern American library is complete without them.

(additional orders of A Home In Bohemia are welcome too - of course.)

```
name_____street_____
city_____state_____zip_____
shipping: allow $1.00 for first book and 50 cents for each
additional book (4th class postal rate) plus $1.00 packaging.
title_____amount_____
title_____amount_____
title_____amount_____
                                          total_____
```